WITCHES OF
NORTHAMPTONSHIRE

WITCHES OF
NORTHAMPTONSHIRE

GARY POOLE

AND

KAREN STOKES

TEMPUS

First published 2006
Reprinted 2007

Tempus Publishing
Cirencester Road, Chalford,
Stroud, Gloucestershire, GL6 8PE
www.tempus-publishing.com

Tempus Publishing is an imprint of NPI Media Group

British Library Cataloguing in Publication Data.
A catalogue record for this book is available from the British Library.

ISBN 978 07524 3980 8

Typesetting and origination by Tempus Publishing Limited.
Printed in Great Britain.

Contents

Acknowledgements

The authors would like to thank all the people that helped with this project, without whom this would have been impossible. It is refreshing to find in this day and age that there are some great people all willing to share their time and knowledge.

A big thank you goes to the Northampton Central Museum, especially Victoria Davies and Rebecca Shawcross, for their patience and understanding, the staff of Lamport Hall, Northampton Record Office for their collection of the Isham Papers and the parish records, Northampton Central Library for a fascinating collection of books and shelter from the cold weather and to Little Billing church, in particular Mr Brian Rogers. During our research we came across many churches that are little gems; please continue your support for these often- forgotten buildings, it would be a shame to lose them. We would like to say a special thank you to Katherine Burton, Ed Palmer, Nicola Guy, Claire Forbes and everybody at Tempus Publishing, who were constantly on hand and helped us when things were tough.

And finally, a massive 'thank you' to our long-suffering family for spending the last six months looking at the back of our heads and for giving us their continued support. Thanks, we couldn't have done it without you.

Introduction

Having both been born and brought up in East Haddon, Northamptonshire we have always been interested in the history of our county and always had the thought that maybe, one day, we could put pen to paper and write a book about some aspect of the county. In recent years we have also developed an interest in the way people have been treated through the ages in regard to their beliefs, specifically those convicted of witchcraft. We live in a time where witches and witchcraft appear regularly on our televisions and at the cinema, although little thought is given to the persecution they had to endure in the past. Today to call someone a witch is a mild insult, but at one time it could be a death sentence. The common Halloween image of an old woman with hunched back, warts and crooked nose is a representation that has carried through time from the early illustrations of the sixteenth century to the well-known film *The Wizard of Oz*.

We thought this would be an ideal opportunity to combine our interests and try and find out as much as we could. We will look at the laws and punishments that were introduced to eliminate witchcraft, as well as the places and people involved in the cases, from the prosecuted people to the people who had the power at that particular time, as well as a bit of social history.

We will also look at the myths and superstitions that surround witchcraft, some of which are still followed to this day, to provide an interesting journey through Northamptonshire's past. Although there does not seem to be much in the way of documentary evidence in many of the cases of suspected witchcraft, we hope that we have covered them all and not missed anyone out!

one

A History of Witchcraft

The history of witchcraft dates back to biblical times with man using magical rites to ensure a successful hunt as far back as the prehistoric era. In Europe the ancient Greeks and Romans recognised the existence of witchcraft. Roman law made distinctions between good magic and harmful magic, with the latter punishable by death. As Christianity spread, all witchcraft was deemed as heresy and the Church set out to stamp it out completely. In England it was not recognized as a mainstream problem until the late fifteenth century when the witch hunts began in earnest, and due to this fact, and also because this book is focused on witchcraft in Northamptonshire, we will only cover the history of witchcraft in England and Central Europe that has a bearing on our county.

It is widely believed that the witch hunts began because of a papal bull (a special charter issued by the Pope), *Summis desiderantes affectibus*, issued by Pope Innocent VIII on 5 December 1484. In this document the Pope recognized different evil practices performed by witches. It dealt, amongst other things, with the witches' intercourse with incubi and succubi and the damage they caused to cattle and livestock. The papal bull also gave power to two inquisitors, Heinrich Kramer and Jacob Sprenger, to hunt out alleged witchcraft throughout Germany. This bull led to one of the severest witch hunts in European history, and Kramer and Springer went onto write one of the main tools of the witch hunter, the '*Malleus maleficarum*'.

A modern translation of the bull says:

It has indeed lately come to Our ears, not without afflicting Us with bitter sorrow, that in some parts of Northern Germany, as well as in the provinces, townships, territories, districts, and dioceses of Mainz, Cologne, Tréves, Salzburg, and Bremen, many persons of both sexes, unmindful of their own salvation and straying from the Catholic Faith, have abandoned themselves to devils, incubi and succubi, and by their incantations, spells, conjurations, and other accursed charms and crafts, enormities and horrid offences, have slain infants yet in the mother's womb, as also the offspring of cattle, have blasted the produce of the earth, the grapes of the vine, the fruits of the trees, nay, men and women, beasts of burthen, herd-beasts, as well as animals of other kinds, vineyards, orchards, meadows, pasture-land, corn, wheat, and all other cereals.

Another important piece of literature was published in Germany in 1486.

The *Malleus Maleficarum*, or 'The Witches Hammer', was a manual written by the two Dominican inquisitors Kramer and Sprenger. It was considered to be the guidebook for inquisitors, and was designed to help them recognise the signs of witchcraft. Montague Summers, who translated it in 1928, called it, 'One of the most important, wisest and weightiest books in the world.' Versions of his translated copy are still available today. During the main period of the witch hunts it was second only in sales to the Bible, until John Bunyan's *Pilgrim's Progress* overtook it in 1678.

Sprenger and Kramer used the Pope's 1484 papal bull as a preface, followed by a letter from four teachers at Cologne University positively recommending it. The letter was in fact a forgery, and the authors were condemned by the Inquisition in 1490. This, however, did nothing to slow the popularity of the book, and it remained in print. The book is divided into three sections, the first proving the existence of witchcraft and sorcery, mainly focusing on the fact that women are more susceptible to the lure of the Devil; the second describes the various forms witchcraft can take, as well as dealing with familiars, and finally the third deals with the detection, trial and execution of witches.

The question asked in Part II, Question I, Chapter III of Montague Summers' translation is, 'how are they transported from place to place? The reply:

> They take the unguent which, as we have said, they make at the Devil's instruction from the limbs of children, particularly of those whom they have killed before baptism, and anoint with it a chair or a broomstick; whereupon they are immediately carried up into the air, either by day or by night, and either visibly or, if they wish, invisibly.

Questions like this did nothing to help those accused of witchcraft, as it is an impossible argument to win. The witch-finders definitely found a use for this publication, and it continued to be referred to as a means of identifying witches for the next 300 years.

In England it was not until 1542 that King Henry VIII issued the first recognised Witchcraft Act. There was an Act passed in 1401 by Archbishop Thomas Arundel called *De haeretico comburendo*, which specifically named *sortilegium*, or sorcery, as heresy, but although this claimed that any witch who did not renounce their beliefs was to be burnt at the stake, this was more of an ecclesiastical law used by the Inquisition and was not really used in the English common court.

When Henry introduced the Act it was at a time of increasing religious tension. On 2 May 1536, only a few years earlier, his second wife Anne Boleyn had been accused of using witchcraft to trap him into marriage and enticing five other men into entering into affairs with her. She was also charged with trying to cause his death. One of the five men, Marc Smeaton, gave a confession – possibly due to torture – that led to Anne's arrest and imprisonment in the Tower of London. On the 17 May the marriage was annulled, although as the records are no longer extant, the stated reason is unknown. Two days later she was beheaded. Henry's Act provided the death penalty to those found guilty of witchcraft and sorcery but only lasted five years, being repealed in 1547 by Henry's son Edward VI.

In 1563 the witch hunt hysteria really began in England, although never on the same scale as in the rest of Europe. The Witchcraft Act issued by Queen Elizabeth I was brought in due to the fear of witchcraft that was sweeping Europe, it carried on from where the earlier Witchcraft Act of 1542 had begun, although it was nowhere near as severe as the legislation in Europe. Elizabeth was widely thought to have been influenced by some of her bishops, who had witnessed first-hand some of the European trials and burnings. It was also rumoured that there were witchcraft plots against her. Witchcraft was now a major crime punishable by death. Those found guilty of murder by witchcraft and sorcery were now hanged until dead, with other lesser instances punished by use of the pillory.

Image of John Dee from Charles Knight, *Old England: A Pictorial Museum*, 1845.

A more severe version of this Act was bought in seventeen years later in 1580, featuring a clause that made it illegal to say or write anything malicious about the Queen or to set down in, 'expresse Wordes Deedes or Writinges, howe longe her Matie shall lyve or contynue, or who shall raigne as King or Queene of this Realme of England after her Highenesse Decease'.

John Dee, one of the counsellors to Elizabeth, was involved in sorcery and had at one time been imprisoned in Hampton Court on charges of witchcraft. Dee was born in 1527 in Mortlake, London, and by the age of fifteen he had entered St John's College, Cambridge where he quickly built a reputation as a mathematician, philosopher and astrologer. By his early twenties his skills had become so renowned that he began drawing up astrological charts for Mary Tudor, the fiercely Catholic Queen who had come to the throne in 1553.

Unfortunately for Dee, the fear of the supernatural and witchcraft was rife, and when he made the mistake of presenting Mary with an unfavourable horoscope, she charged him with witchcraft and imprisoned him at Hampton Court. Although he was acquitted of the charge, he remained in prison until 1555. In 1558, Dee's fortunes took an upturn. Mary died, and her Protestant sister Elizabeth came to the throne, immediately consulting Dee on the best astrological date for her coronation. A friendly relationship blossomed between Dee and the new Queen, and Elizabeth kept him permanently in the wings, not wishing to be seen by the court openly liaising with a suspected sorcerer.

By 1581 Dee reported having many strange dreams and hearing disturbing noises in his house. Convinced that spirits were trying to contact him he began crystal-gazing, or scrying, to communicate with them. He unfortunately had little success with this, and decided to employ the services of one Edward Kelley, who acted as a medium, communicating with the spirits through the means of a crystal ball.

In 1585, Dee and Kelley went on a four-year journey across the Continent conducting readings for nobility and royalty, but as the fear of heresy spread across Europe they never stayed long in any one place. Dee and Kelley eventually parted ways, Dee returning to England while Kelley remained in Europe to continue his opulent lifestyle. In May of 1591, Kelley was arrested and imprisoned in the castle of Purglitz near Prague on the orders of Rudolf II for failing to

Edward Kelly [*sic*] in the act of invoking the spirit of a Deceased, from Ebenezer Sibly's *Astrology by Sibly*, 1806.

live up to his promises; he had convinced Rudolf he could produce gold by means of alchemy. Kelley was killed in 1595 at the age of forty-two while attempting to escape from the prison. The story goes that he died because he used an insufficiently long rope to lower himself from a tower when he fell, broke his legs and died from his injuries.

Dee went on to write many books on the supernatural and the occult, but after the death of Elizabeth – and with her successor King James' hatred of all things to do with witchcraft and the occult – he returned to Mortlake, where he spent his final years living in extreme poverty, dying at the age of eighty-one in 1608. He is believed to have inspired the character of Prospero in William Shakespeare's *The Tempest*, and also the main character in Christopher Marlowe's *Dr Faustus*. His crystal ball and magical equipment can be seen at the British Museum.

Not everybody in the period believed in witchcraft. Reginald Scott was the first English writer to publish a major work on the subject. His book, *The Discoverie of Witchcraft* (1584), set out to show that belief in witchcraft was mere superstition and a sign of a poor faith in God. Scott describes the look of witches in Book I, Chapter III of his book as: 'women which be commonly old, lame, blear-eyed, pale, foul, and full of wrinkles; poor, and sullen, superstitious, and papists; or such as know no religion'. He goes on to say:

These miserable wretches are so odious unto all their neighbours, and so feared, as few dare offend them, or deny them any thing they ask: whereby they take upon them; yea, and sometimes think, that they can do such things as are beyond the ability of human nature. These go from house to house, and from door to door for a pot full of milk, yeast, drink, pottage, or some such relief; without the which they could hardly live: neither obtaining for their service and pains, nor by their art, nor yet at the Devils hands (with whom they are said to make a perfect and visible bargain) either beauty, money, promotion, wealth, worship, pleasure, honor, knowledge, learning, or any other benefit whatsoever.

Born 1538 in Kent to rich Protestant parents, he attended Hart College in Oxford, though he never received a degree. He was well known for his clearness of thinking and compassion; this was rare in this period of history, and when he published *Discoverie* it caused quite an uproar among the general population. In the book he was very critical of the Catholic Church and blamed them for the current popular obsession with witchcraft. Scott's book was widely condemned, to the point where King James ordered all copies to be burnt. Like *Malleus Maleficarum*, Scott's book is still widely available today despite all James did to destroy it.

Cotta's book *The Trial of Witchcraft*, published in 1616, may well have been in response to the 1612 witch trials held in Northampton. After the death of Elizabeth in 1603, King James I (VI of Scotland) came to the throne, becoming the first king to rule England, Scotland and Ireland at the same time. He referred to his kingdom as 'Great Britain'. The son of Mary Queen of Scots, James was highly intellectual and religious. He was responsible for writing several books, one of which was *Daemonologie* (1597), influenced by his serious obsession with destroying witchcraft. He wrote it in the form of a dialogue between Philomathes and Episteman. In the preface to the reader he explains that the book is written as an answer to Reginald Scott and German physician Johann Wierus's earlier books denying the existence of witchcraft. The book is divided into three parts, with the first dealing with magic in general, 'and necromancie in special', the second discusses sorcery and witchcraft, with the last covering the subject of spirits and familiars.

In 1604, James introduced a more severe witchcraft act and broadening Elizabeth's earlier act, it now allowed the death penalty for anybody seen to invoke evil spirits or commune with spirits or familiars. He was also responsible for authorising the publication of the most recognized translation of the Bible in the same year.

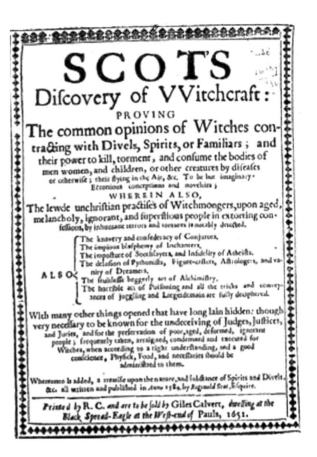

The cover of Reginald Scots' *Discovery of Witchcraft*.

William Shakespeare, the King's favourite playwright, wrote the tragedy *Macbeth* around 1606. Featuring three witches, it was generally thought to be based on James' ancestor Malcolm. His descision to write *Macbeth* was probably due to James granting him a title, as well as the King's (and the general public's) current fascination with witchcraft.

Witch-finders were a very important part of the witch trial process; sometimes they were officials appointed by the courts but often they were independent entrepreneurs out to make a living from the identification of witches. They often gained a great deal of enjoyment from the pursuit of witches, not to mention the monetary aspect involved. They studied all the documents available at the time, the main 'bible' being the *Malleus Maleficarum*, to better acquaint themselves with the facts about witchcraft and improve their chances of catching their prey.

The witch-finders often supplied the investigators with the information they required to start the trial process, although they tended not to get involved in the actual trials. The information they supplied would often have come from observing the villages and towns and listening to local gossip, looking for the slightest indication of witchcraft. It was not unknown for them to travel from town to town in the hope of uncovering a witch, although in an area where witchcraft was suspected they would often be called in by the local authority.

Witch finding was a well-paid profession and they were often paid according to their rate of success and it was therefore very important for them to find evidence of witchcraft. They would rarely leave an area without identifying a witch and would be more than happy to use all the methods at their disposal. Swimming was a favoured method, believed to be used for the first time in England in 1612 at Northampton. Once a supposed witch was identified and sentenced to stand trial they would quickly move on to another area in the hope of earning more money. It was very rare for people of high standing or people popular in the local community to be accused and it tended to be persons of relatively poor social standing or social outcasts.

England's most notorious witch-finder was the 'Witch-Finder General' Matthew Hopkins, and it has been documented that both he and his assistant John Stearne visited Northamptonshire amongst other counties including Suffolk, Cambridgeshire, Huntingdonshire and most of East Anglia. He was well acquainted with *Daemonologie,* and used this as a guide for his actions. Matthew Hopkins, the son of James Hopkins – the rector of Wenham in Suffolk – was born between 1619 and 1622. He moved from Suffolk to Manningtree, Essex at the age of twenty and is believed to have suffered from tuberculosis. Little is known of his education as no records show him attending school or university but, judging from his later life and writings, he could read and write Latin and English, so therefore he must have received an adequate education. He had also acquired some knowledge of maritime law having worked for a time as a clerk for a shipowner at Mistley in Essex.

Hopkins' career as a witch hunter began at the Thorn Inn in Mistley in 1644. He had no official qualifications for the job, though he did have an unquestioning belief that his actions were righteous. His first victim was one-legged Elizabeth Clarke from Manningtree. She was old and thought strange by the local villagers, thus making her an ideal candidate for being accused of witchcraft. She was soon tortured into giving a confession and admitted to consorting with the Devil and to having familiars. She went on to name other witches in the local area, who went on to name others in turn and within a short while thirty-eight people had been accused, with many local people giving credence to Hopkins' evidence. His career was off to a flying start: so much so that he hired an assistant, John Stearne, and went on to hire four more, helping him to extend his witch-finding empire to the surrounding counties.

Hopkins and Stearne felt they were performing a public service. They denied that they were money orientated and instead cited that they put themselves at risk with their work, and that they were welcomed wherever they went, they only received money as a thank you and as recompense. Records show that within two years Hopkins had earned the modern-day equivalent of £60,000.

Hopkins used torture on a regular basis in the obtaining of confessions, and he and his assistants were capable of phrasing questions in such a way during interrogations that it was almost impossible for the accused not to incriminate themselves. He accused people of the standard witchcraft crimes: death or injury to people and livestock, keeping familiars and using broomsticks to fly, but his favourite accusation was the crime of signing a pact with the Devil.

By the spring of 1646 Hopkins and Stearne found themselves in Northamptonshire and the surrounding counties. According to John Stearne's own book of 1648, *A Confirmation and Discovery of Witchcraft*, one 'Cherrie' of Thrapston, 'a very aged man', was accused of bewitching a neighbour after an argument over some cattle. Cherrie apparently 'wished that his tongue would rot out of his head'; shortly after the man did become ill and, according to Stearne, 'his tongue did come out of his mouth, hanging only by its roots.' Subsequently the man died. Cherrie went on to confess to this, as well as two other cases of causing death by bewitchment. He was also asked questions about the livestock of local landowner Sir John Washington, who had lost numerous cattle in apparently strange circumstances, he pleaded guilty to causing their deaths.

When asked why he had caused distress to Washington, a man who had been nothing but kind to him in the past, he replied: 'The more he gave him, the more power he had over him to do mischief, for he said his Imps must be employed else they would not let him be quiet, but torment him.' Stearne goes on to say that Cherrie had admitted to making a pact with the

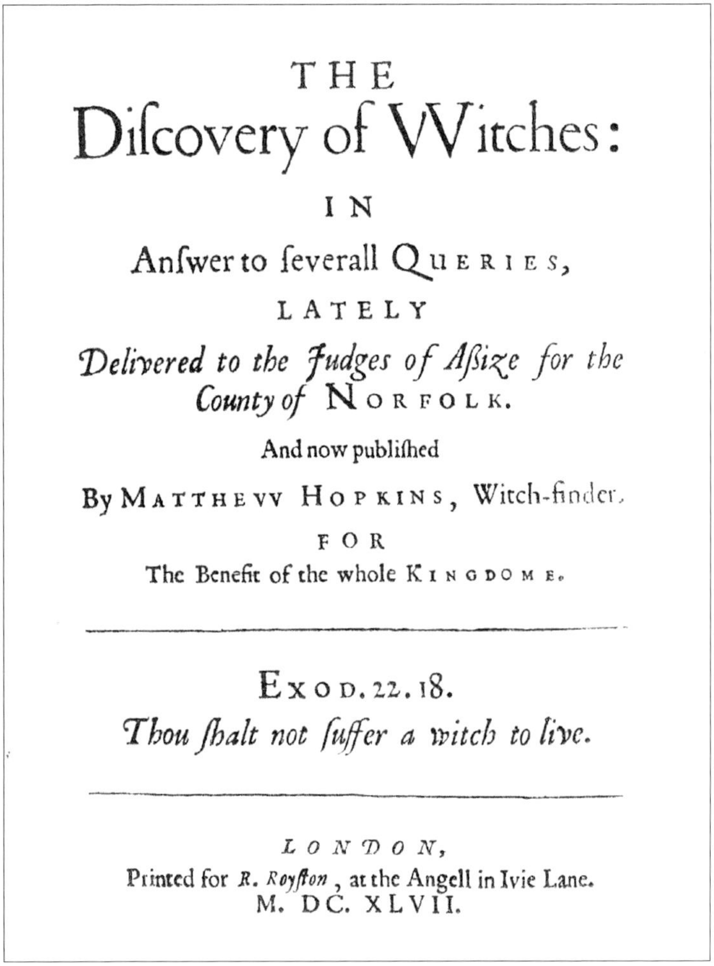

THE

Diſcovery of Witches:

I N

Anſwer to ſeverall Q U E R I E S,

L A T E L Y

*Delivered to the Judges of Aſſize for the
County of* N O R F O L K.

And now publiſhed

By M A T T H E vv   H O P K I N S , Witch-finder.

F O R

The Benefit of the whole K I N G D O M E.

E X O D. 22. 18.
Thou ſhalt not ſuffer a witch to live.

L O N D O N,
Printed for *R. Royſton* , at the Angell in Ivie Lane.
M. D C. X L V I I.

The cover of *Discovery
of Witches* by Matthew
Hopkins.

Devil and using imps to do his bidding. He was indicted by grand jury, but died in gaol on the very day he was to have been tried.

John Stearne goes on to mention three more cases from Northamptonshire in his book, that of John Wynnick, also of Thrapston, and Anne Goodfellow of Woodford, although both of these were tried in Huntingdonshire in April/May 1646, and a small entry on an unknown young man of Denford who confessed to sending imps to worry the cattle of a Mr Cocke, also of Denford.

John Wynnick was accused that while working in a hay barn he lost a purse containing seven shillings, which sent him into such a rage he called on the Devil for help. Apparently, the Devil duly appeared in the shape of a bear and told him that if he was to worship him his money would be returned the following day. This did indeed happen, and Wynnick confessed in his trial that in return for worshipping the Devil his wishes would be granted. He was found guilty and hanged. Anne Goodfellow was also found guilty of making a pact with the Devil, but in this instance he appeared in the shape of a white cat. He again promised that wishes would be fulfilled, but in her confession she claimed the Devil a liar as many of the things she wanted remained unobtainable. Goodfellow suffered a similar fate to that of Wynnick.

Revd John Gaule, minister at Great Staughton in Huntingdonshire, publicly spoke out against Hopkins and his assistants in April 1646, claiming no innocent old woman was safe from accusations – this caused Hopkins to write the pamphlet *The Discovery of Witches* in 1647 in defence of himself and his methods. After writing the pamphlet little is known of what became of Hopkins. John Stearne explained in 1648 that Hopkins had always suffered bad health and had died of consumption in Manningtree in 1647. Despite this claim much speculation surrounded the seeming disappearance of Hopkins. There were many myths regarding his death, one being that he himself was accused of witchcraft and subsequently was submitted to the swimming test his guilt being shown by the fact that he floated, he was then chased out of town. Another myth claims that he was hanged. Whatever the explanation for his demise, one thing beyond all doubt is that during his short career Hopkins and his assistants were responsible for the conviction or execution of at least 230 alleged witches.

According to many records the execution of Elinor Shaw and Mary Phillips in 1705 was the last case of execution for witchcraft in England. There was a later case, that of Ruth Osborne from Tring in 1750, who was suspected of bewitching a neighbour named Butterfield because, during the rebellion of 1745, he had refused her request for buttermilk, but she died from the effects of cruelty while being dunked. The story goes that Butterfield, a publican, sent for a white (or harmless) witch from Northampton, who confirmed that he had indeed been cursed by Ruth Osborne. In an effort to remove the curse it was suggested that six locals, armed with pitchforks and charms as a security against evil spirits, guarded Butterfield's house. This came at a great cost with no visible improvement to his health. A group of his customers decided to take matters into their own hands by sending a notice round the nearby market towns promising there would be a ducking on Monday 22 April, 1750. At Tring on the arranged day a mob of 10,000 people gathered to take Ruth Osborne and her husband to be ducked – they were dragged two miles to the nearest pond at Marlston Mere, stripped naked, tied and dunked in the water. The old woman died from the effects of the cruelty. (One of her tormentors, a chimney sweep named Colley who had been noticeably brutal during the whole process, was later chained and hanged the following year.)

The outrage that this event (and others like it) caused led to a rethink of the laws dealing with witchcraft but, as will be seen, they were not always followed. In 1735 George II had issued an Act repealing the earlier Witchcraft Acts of Elizabeth I and James I. The penalties were relaxed and the death penalty abolished, only stating:

> That if any Person shall, from and after the said Twenty-fourth Day of June, pretend to exercise or use any kind of Witchcraft, Sorcery, Inchantment, or Conjuration, or undertake to tell Fortunes, or pretend, from his or her Skill or Knowledge in any occult or crafty Science, to discover where or in what manner any Goods or Chattels, supposed to have been stolen or lost, may be found, every Person, so offending, being thereof lawfully convicted on Indictment or Information in that part of Great Britain called England, or on Indictment or Libel in that part of Great Britain called Scotland, shall, for every such Offence, suffer Imprisonment by the Space of one whole Year without Bail or Mainprize, and once in every Quarter of the said Year, in some Market Town of the proper County, upon the Market Day, there stand openly on the Pillory by the Space of One Hour.

It is widely believed that the witch hunts came to an end during this 'period of Enlightenment' because of man's natural progression. It was a time of rising knowledge in the field of science and many of mankind's superstitions and his general ignorance was being replaced by rationalism.

Even as late as 1944 the Witchcraft Act was enforced. Helen Duncan, a Scottish psychic, was the last person to be convicted under the Act. Authorities feared that by her alleged clairvoyant

Matthew Hopkins, from his pamphlet *The Discovery of Witches*, printed in London in 1647.

powers she could betray details of the D-Day preparations. During a séance in Portsmouth she had indicated knowledge that HMS *Barham* had been sunk, which had at the time been kept from the public. Although Prime Minister Winston Churchill openly commented about the 'obsolete tomfoolery' of the trial, she still spent nine months in prison.

It was not until 22 June, 1951 that the final Witchcraft Act was repealed in England. The Witchcraft Act of 1735 was replaced by the Fraudulent Mediums Act. Witchcraft was now no longer illegal, and after hundreds of years of people denying being witches the repeal led to Gerald Gardner, a retired civil servant originally from Liverpool, writing *Witchcraft Today*. He and others like him, Doreen Valiente and Aleister Crowley to name but two, openly admitted to being witches and legally formed covens. Gerald Gardner was responsible for starting the Wicca movement which is now well established throughout Europe and America.

The repeal also allowed Cecil Hugh Williamson to open the famous 'Museum of Magic and Witchcraft' at Castletown, in the Isle of Man, which was later closed and its contents sold to the 'Ripley's, believe it or not' organization in America in 1996. In America in 1985, as a result of a court case, the District Court of Virginia ruled that Wicca is a legally recognized religion and is afforded all the benefits accorded to it by law. How times change!

The period when witch-hunting was at its peak was often called 'the burning times', and although no exact figures can be given it is believed that no more than 5,000 trials for witchcraft took place in Britain during this time. The total number of executions has been estimated as less than 2,500.

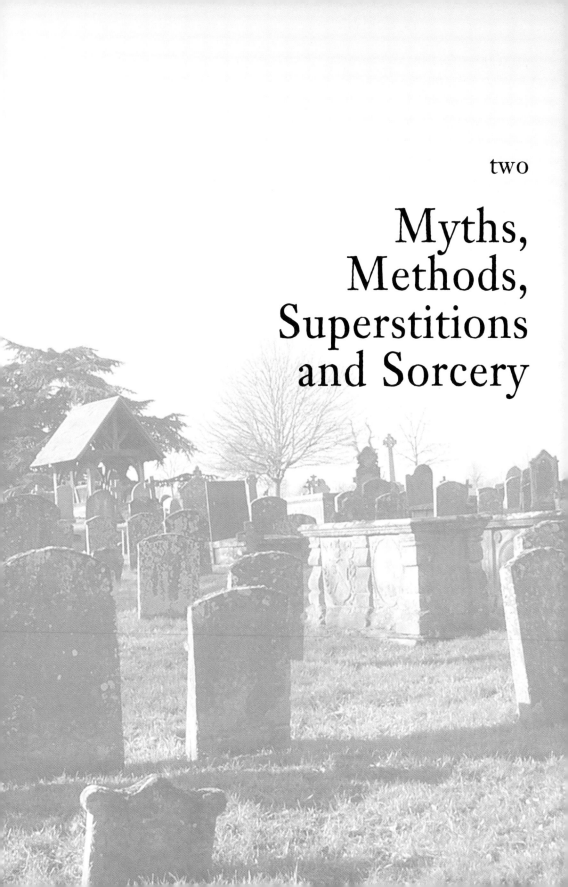

two

Myths,
Methods,
Superstitions
and Sorcery

This section alphabetically shows the methods of punishment and some of the many myths and superstitions that surrounded witchcraft in England.

ALL HALLOW'S EVE

All Hallow's Eve or Halloween is celebrated on the night of 31 October. Halloween is one of the times of the year when the spirit world can make contact with the physical world and when magic is most potent.

APPEARANCE

Everyone has their own idea of how they imagine a witch to look. This is as true today as it was in the past. If an old woman lived alone, was ugly or misshapen and was seen to show strange patterns of behaviour, for example talking to herself, this was often enough to make them a target and be seen as a witch. The common image shown throughout England in illustrations of old women made them very vulnerable to the methods used for the extraction of confessions. These women may already have been in poor health, either mentally or physically, and at the time of torture were likely to agree to anything in the hope of ending the punishment.

BLOOD

It was a common belief that a witch's power could be broken by the drawing of their blood. The blood was drawn by scratching above the mouth or nose. This method was used by angry mobs as well as those in local authority. Victims of witchcraft were known to boil their own blood over a hot fire, whilst reciting incantations at midnight. The hot blood would then be thrown onto the coals. This caused pain and discomfort to the witch, forcing them to lift the spell.

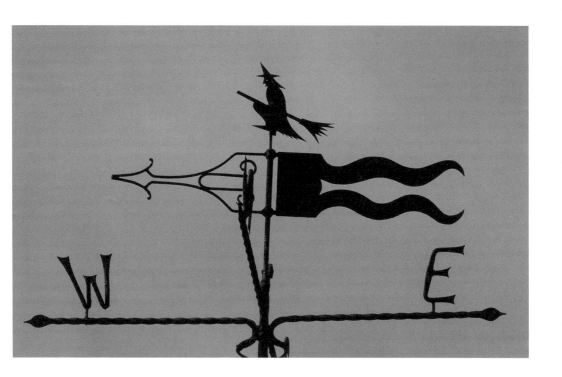

Above: A weathervane from a house in Kingsthorpe.

Right: French illustration of a witch.

BODKINS AND AWLS

The bodkin and awl were small, sharply pointed instruments for making holes in fabric or leather. The awl in particular was a favourite tool used by witch-finder Matthew Hopkins when testing witches by pricking. Hopkins is reputed to have used fake bodkins, which were hollow-handled instruments that would allow the point to retract, and needles with one blunt end were used to show areas that produced no pain or blood.

CAULDRON

The cauldron was an iron pot used in most homes throughout history for cooking and boiling over an open fire. A broth or stew would be made with items added daily; it depended on what the home owner could find or what was in season. It is however heavily associated with witchcraft and features in *Macbeth* (Act IV Scene I):

> Double, double toil and trouble;
> Fire burn, and cauldron bubble.

This an integral part of the witch myth, with witches often portrayed stirring vile brews featuring ingredients such as eye-of-newt and toe-of-frog. They are often believed to boil small children too. Witches used their cauldron for brewing potions and ointments, and this is still the case with modern neo-pagan witches who follow Wicca although their use is more for burning incense and as a decoration in the home. A mid-eighteenth century example of a cauldron can be seen at the Northampton Museum at Abington, once the site of the first gallows in Northamptonshire.

CAUSING DEATH, INJURY OR DAMAGE BY WITCHCRAFT

In most trials it was common to be accused of using witchcraft to kill someone. It was not always necessary to be anywhere near the victim when death occurred and matters were made worse if the witch had reason for disliking the deceased. In some cases if illness or injury had affected a neighbour or livestock this would be as strong a case as if a death had occurred. If people were stricken with fits, hens stopped laying, cows failed to give milk or crops failed charges for witchcraft would often follow.

CHARGES OF WITCHCRAFT

The reasons for people to be charged with witchcraft were often very dubious. It was very difficult to prove that the accused were witches; unfortunately, the courts were not always worried about proof and sentenced many people on the tiniest amount of evidence. A neighbour's account and forced confession was usually enough, an overzealous witch-finder or a feud with a neighbour was all it took for charges to be laid.

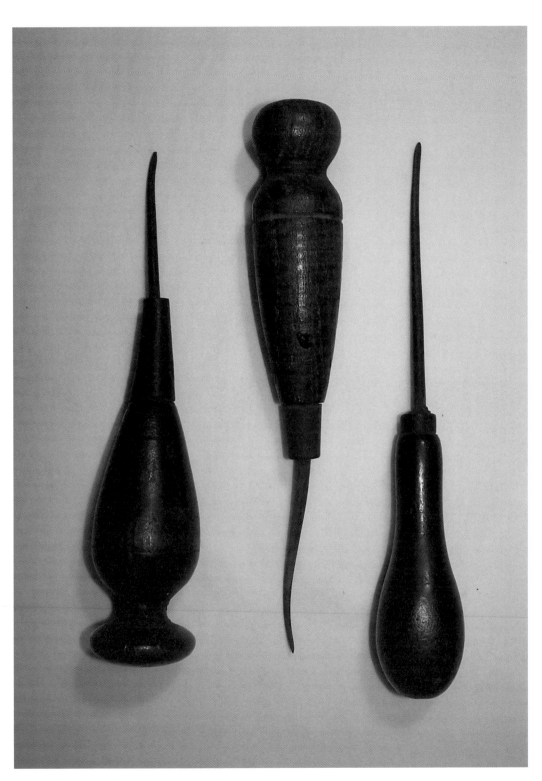

Awls from the Northampton Central Museum.

Above: Woodcut of a baby in a cauldron.

Left: Witches around a cauldron.

Cauldron from the Northampton Abington Museum.

CHILDBIRTH

Before maternity hospitals were built and childbirth took place in the home precautions were taken to ease the pains and ensure safe delivery. All the doors in the home were unlocked and all knots loosened as a defence against witchcraft as it was believed witches tied knots to prevent delivery.

CHURCHES

Many of Northamptonshire's churches contain references to witchcraft and to the people mentioned in this book.

Barton Seagrave

The church was refashioned by medieval builders who blocked up the Norman windows and replaced the south wall of the Norman nave with their own arcade. Despite the changes over the years the Norman font still remains having staples around the edge as a way to lock it against witches. Witch staples were employed to protect the holy water from witches who were believed to hold the keys to life and death.

Little Billing

All Saints church is set in a picturesque sandstone hamlet on the banks of the river Nene, which, in the Saxon and medieval periods, would have been of significant strategic and economic importance due to its location near the river crossing at Clifford Hill. The church continued to grow until the sixteenth century then entered a gradual decline which was halted in the nineteenth century when it was restored. Unfortunately, this restoration removed much of the stone work and evidence of the earlier church.

The oldest remaining part of this church is its early sandstone Norman/Saxon font, which dates from around AD 1000. Barrel-shaped, it features an unfinished Latin inscription around it which is still easy to read: '*Wigberhtus artifex atq cementarius huic fabricavit [...] quisquis suum venit mergere corpus procul dubio caeit [...]*', which translates as, 'Wighbert the craftsman and mason made this [...] Whoever comes to dip his body without doubt gains [...]'. The font was also fitted with a lock and staple as protection against witchcraft and the remnants of this can still be seen.

Nassington

This thirteenth-century font with ivy leaves on the stem and rosettes on the base also features witch staples.

Syresham

The Wesleyan chapel contains an inscription to the memory of John Kurde which reads, 'In memory of John Kurde, shoemaker, the Syresham martyr, burnt at the stake in defence of the truth, 1667. Tell ye your children of it, and let your children tell their children, and their children another generation'.

Titchmarsh

This thirteenth-century church contains monuments to the Pickering family. Some of the walls still contain part of the paintings of Mrs Creed, John Dryden's cousin (Dryden was the first official Poet Laureate) and the only daughter of Sir Gilbert Pickering. Sir Gilbert bought the manor house in Titchmarsh in the sixteenth century. Mrs Creed was also a cousin of Samuel Pepys and frequently appears in his diary. The church also features the Pickering family pew in the room above the porch. Other churches whose fonts feature witch staples are Cranford St Andrew, Duddington, Flore, Pitsford, Roade, and Ufford.

CONCEALED SHOES

The importance of these items is not exactly known. There are a few theories however, one of them being that they were a fertility symbol, 'there was an old woman who lived in a shoe, she had so many children she didn't know what to do!' Another is that they were a charm against witchcraft and evil spirits. This seems to stem from one of England's 'unofficial saints', John Schorn, a rector of North Marston (1290-1314), Buckingham, who was reputed to have trapped the Devil in a boot, leading people to believe that concealing a boot or shoe would act as a trap for any evil spirits or unwanted intruders such as witches.

The most common places these items are found are in chimneys, under floorboards and in roofs. They have also been found in bricked-up ovens and around doors and windows. These areas were considered the most vulnerable and were most likely to be the place where a witch or an evil spirit would enter the home. Almost all of the shoes found are extremely well worn and have been repeatedly repaired, because, for most people, shoes were the most expensive item of clothing and consequently were worn and constantly repaired until they almost fell to bits. Indeed, some of the concealed shoes found are that well worn and so much beyond repair it's difficult to tell whether they were man, woman or child's.

All Saints church, Little Billing.

The Little Billing font.

A staple on Little Billing's font.

Although both men's and women's boots and shoes have been discovered, over half of the finds have been children's, the belief being that the shoe held the spirit of the person wearing it and a child's spirit was a lot purer and therefore would be more of a deterrent to evil spirits and wicked witches. In most cases single shoes are found, sometimes in family groups, (the father's, mother's and a child's) but pairs are rare. Other items are often found with the shoe, ranging from knives, bowls and spoons to purses and bones (these tend to be chicken bones for the most part but some have been cat bones, the significance of which is open to speculation). As with the shoes these items are usually damaged in some way, again the reason is rather a mystery.

The Northampton Museum is the world's largest shoe museum and also holds the largest collection of concealed shoes, ranging in date from the early fifteenth century up to the late nineteenth century. It seems wherever British people settled this superstition was carried out. Examples have been found all over Britain and as far away as Canada and the United States. Over 1,600 shoes have to date been recorded at the Northampton Museum, with more being reported every week.

DEVIL'S PACT

The pledge with the Devil was sometimes verbally agreed but usually signed in blood from the witch's left hand on virgin parchment paper. The pact was signed declaring allegiance with the Devil in return for help with the witch's magic in any way required. Familiars were often supplied as part of the deal to aid the witches and carry out their wishes. Another theory is that the pact was signed giving the Devil your soul in return for wealth and power, etc.

Concealed items found at Watling Street, Towcester. (Courtesy Northampton Central Museum)

Concealed items found at St Peter's House, Brackley. (Courtesy Northampton Central Museum)

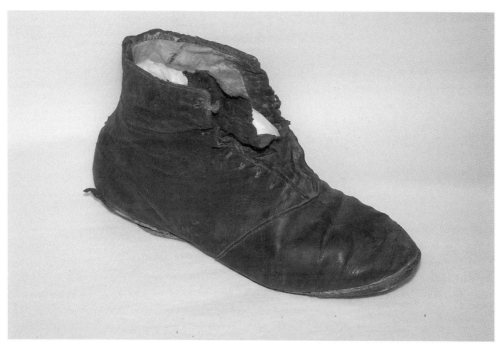

Concealed shoe from unknown location within the county. (Courtesy Northampton Central Museum)

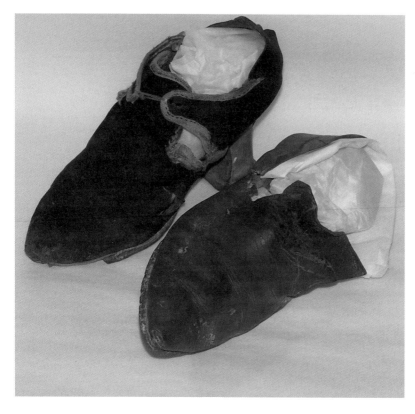

Concealed shoes from unknown location within the county. (Courtesy Northampton Central Museum)

Witch-hunting manuals such as the *Malleus Maleficarum* discussed pacts in great detail and these guidelines were followed by witch-hunters such as Matthew Hopkins, who obtained sworn evidence of written pacts. Whether any of his 230-plus victims were condemned purely on this evidence is unknown, but after the third Parliamentary Witchcraft Act of 1604 it became illegal to make pacts with any evil spirit and became a major part of the trials that were to follow.

EXECUTION

English courts usually ordered those found guilty of witchcraft to be hanged while the method of burning alive was saved for those found guilty of treason. Therefore the case of Elinor Shaw and Mary Phillips is quite a rarity, as they were sentenced to be hanged and then burnt. Burning at the stake was a painful death, especially if the wood used was green as this would be slow to burn resulting in a slow, agonising death.

Executions of witches were seen as a major public occasion and large crowds would gather to witness the spectacle. The accused were usually expected to repeat their confession or, if they pleaded not guilty, were expected to repent their sins and confess anew in front of the crowd. The executions in Northampton generally took place on a Saturday not long after the sentencing, with the locals notified by the tolling of church bells. Record has it that like the trial and torture all expenses for the execution were paid for by the condemned's estate or by relatives.

Although these were the only two witches mentioned who were burnt at the stake, listed below are individuals executed in the county by the same method, but due to the lack of remaining evidence it is unknown whether any of these were tried as witches or even whether witchcraft was in any way involved. Due to the nature of how they met their death we have included them in this book.

1557	John Kurde, a shoemaker from Syresham – burnt in the stone pits beyond the North Gate of the town for transubstantiation.
1631	Mrs Lucas, of Moulton – burnt for poisoning her husband.
1645	Woman (Unknown) – burnt for poisoning her husband. Executed near Queen's Cross.
1655	Woman (Unknown) – burnt for poisoning her husband. Executed at Boughton Green.
1715	Elizabeth Treslar – hanged then burnt on Northampton Heath.
1735	Elizabeth Fawson – hanged then burnt for poisoning her husband.

Although little is known of the above executions the case of John Kurde and Elizabeth Lawson have been documented.

Kurde was arrested on an act of heresy, that of transubstantiation, meaning that he failed to attend Holy Communion at his parish church and was subsequently imprisoned in Northampton Castle. The trial took place at All Saints church, where he was found guilty and sentenced to be burnt at the stake. He was led out of the town by the North Gate and taken along what we now know as Barrack Road to Kingsthorpe Hollow. At the site of the stone pits (close to the present day Barrack Road Royal Mail Depot) John Roote, the vicar of St Giles, offered to pardon him if he recanted. Kurde simply replied, 'I have my pardon by Jesus Christ'. He was then burnt at the stake.

A detailed account of the execution of Elizabeth Fawson appeared in the *Mercury* of 1735 and explains the procedure for her execution. She was drawn in a sledge to the Northampton

Heath, which is now known as the Racecourse, on the Kettering Road. Here she asked the attending officer to make sure that she was dead before being burnt. According to Taylor & Son's *Northamptonshire Handbook*, 'and being fixed to the stake, and the rope round her neck for some small time, she desired again to be dispatch'd, and accordingly the stool was drawn from under her, and the fire being lighted as directed, in about two or three hours she was entirely consumed'.

FAMILIARS

As well as having the appearance of a witch, another thing that could lead to accusations was having a familiar. A familiar is very much a part of witchcraft folklore but, as can be seen later in this book, it is something that most accused witches were thought to have. Familiars were thought to be demons or imps specifically assigned to the witches by the Devil to assist them with their witchcraft. They often took the form of cats or dogs. Therefore if you were an old lonely woman with a pet cat or, even worse, several cats, this could lead into being accused of witchcraft. To make matters worse it was not always necessary to own a cat or dog to be accused, often, one passing by your door could be enough. The list of animals considered to be familiars includes hares, toads, crows, blackbirds, mice, rats, and even bees.

Traditionally it is thought familiars had the ability to disappear at will as well as being able to change shape. Witches were popularly believed to take good care of their familiars, feeding them well and even rewarding them with drops of their own blood. It was for this purpose that it is believed some witches had third nipples.

Witches were believed to use their familiars to carry out their evil deeds such as turning milk sour or injuring livestock.

FLYING BY BROOMSTICK

It was thought that the broomstick was the preferred form of transport for witches. During the interrogation process carried out to obtain a confession witches were asked whether they flew on broomsticks and admissions to this have been found. It was often reported by neighbours that the accused were seen flying from their windows on broomsticks and this did not help the accused. It does seem strange that if the broomstick was indeed the main form of transport then why did the Guilsborough witches (featured later) choose to travel the small distance of two miles to visit a sick friend on a sow's back?!

The broom would have been found in every house – it was at the time the only way to tidy the house. Witches were believed to have made flying ointments and these were supposedly rubbed into the broomstick. Recipes can still be found for this 'wonder' ointment. One such recipe, taken from *The Complete Incense, Oils & Brews* by Scott Cunningham, lists the ingredients for 'Flying Ointment' as cinquefoil, parsley, aconite, belladonna, hemlock and cowbane, definitely a dangerous group of ingredients.

The most likely reason for the myth of witches riding broomsticks is that through history women straddled the broom and hopped along the ground in the hope of promoting fertility of the fields, and this through time was exaggerated into the myth we now know.

Woodcut from Corbell, near Paris, depicting a witch with familiar. (Taken from *Wright's History of Caricature and Grotesque in Art,* p. 131)

PLANTS AND TREES

Here are a few examples from the many plants and trees that were surrounded by superstition. It is by no means a complete list as this would be a book in its own right. What is of interest is that what was once considered as witchcraft later became known as herbalism, with Nicholas Culpeper releasing his well-known guide to the discoveries and remedies using all things herbal in 1826.

Briony
A climbing herb with thick roots also known as 'Devil's turnip', used by witches as a replacement for mandrake in their spells. Culpeper believed briony to 'purge the belly with great violence,' although he goes on to say that, in moderation, it was 'very profitable for diseases of the head'.

Elder
Elder (*Sambucus Nigra*) has a mixed relationship with witchcraft. It is now seen in the modern Wiccan faith as one of the favourite woods to make wands; however, it is thought by Wiccans to be bad luck to cut it, and it should only be used if the tree spirit agrees or if the branch fell naturally from the tree. In the past the elder tree was viewed differently. Elder trees were thought to contain evil spirits and it was feared that the Devil would enter the home through the chimney if elder was burnt. It was feared to bring death if brought indoors.

Strangely though, it was viewed to have anti-evil properties too, if a dwarf elder bush was cut it would cause injury to any witches in the nearby vicinity. Smearing elder juice on the eyes gave you the ability to see any nearby witch and view what they were doing. As mentioned, elder was not taken indoors, but it would be hung above the door, usually cut on the last day of April, to ward off magic and prevent witches from entering. Amulets shaped from elder or twigs were worn for protection. A Northamptonshire superstition states that warts could be driven away by crossing over them with elder twigs.

Ergot
Ergot (*Claviceps Purpurea*) is a fungus that affects cereal crops and when digested causes hallucinations and convulsions. Rye was especially affected by ergot and this was a common crop in Britain and Colonial America in the sixteenth and seventeenth centuries. The symptoms of 'bewitchment' could be blamed on this fungus-affected rye, as records show that the most prolific areas for witch trials were the very same areas where rye was grown. This could be the reason behind the Warboys and Salem witch trials. Ergot thrives in a cold wet climate and still affects a small amount of crops today.

Rowan

The rowan tree (*Sorbus Aucuparia*) is known by many names, including mountain ash (although it is not a member of the ash family), witch wood, witch tree and witchbane. The leaves, fruit and wood of the rowan tree were believed to be very effective in combating witchcraft. Rowan would be tied to an animal's halter or placed in the stable or cowshed to prevent horses being ridden by the hags of the night and to stop cows having their udders sucked dry by witch's familiars.

It was common to make butter churns, milking stools and pails from rowan wood to stop the milk from being curdled by a witch's spell, and throughout East Anglia almost all homes, cowsheds, stables and pigsties had rowan twig crosses placed above the door as protection against witchcraft. The twig crosses were sometimes placed above a child's cradle, not only as protection against bewitchment but also to prevent the child from being stolen by fairies. The crosses would be replaced by freshly cut ones each May Day.

It was felt to be lucky to plant a rowan near the home and churchyards contained rowan trees to stop the dead from rising from their graves and to keep away demons. The bright red berries of the rowan were also believed to protect against witchcraft and disease and were sometimes strung together into a necklace and worn by the victims of sorcery.

Hawthorn

Hawthorn (*Crataegus Monogyna*), like elder, is used by witches and against them. Witches used the thorns when stabbing effigies to cause pain, injury or death while hawthorn was planted near the home's entrance to ward off witches, who would be scared of getting caught in the sharp thorns. Hawthorn blossom is as strange, with some people believing it bad luck to bring it indoors while others decorated their homes with the blossom to ward off evil spirits.

Wych Elm

The wood of the wych elm (*Ulmus Montana*), often spelt 'witch', was used very much like rowan. It was thought to be a protection against witchcraft and a small piece of it would be placed in the butter churn to prevent the witch from curdling the butter.

Yew

Yew (*Taxus Baccata*) was considered to provide protection against witchcraft and it was planted in churchyards to protect people from ghosts and evil spirits. Although another theory of why it was placed in churchyards was to keep the cattle grazing nearby from entering the churchyard as the leaves were said to be poisonous. Culpeper contradictorily says of yew, 'a most poisonous vegetable, the berries of which threaten present death to man and beast that eat them: many in this country have eaten them and survived.'

SHAPE-SHIFTING

Mythologies of many cultures refer to their deities' ability to change into animal or human form. Belief that witches possessed the magical ability of transformation was also widespread. Many trials for witchcraft contain references to shape-shifting, with the accused said to have performed evil deeds whilst in the form of animals or birds.

The Encyclopedia of Superstitions mentions a tale relating to shape-shifting. While walking with his son in Syresham, a man cut a stick for the boy and was horribly surprised to see blood gushing from the cut (the actual type of tree is debatable, it is thought that it was elder or oak).

Yew tree in St Andrew's churchyard, Harlestone.

A little while after this event, a local woman suspected of witchcraft was seen with her arm bandaged up and although this would be overlooked today, at this time it was seen as proof that the woman was indeed a witch.

TESTS

Cucking Stool

The cucking stool or stool of repentance dates back to Saxon times and the accused would be tied to a chair and paraded through the streets. Such a stool, called *cathedra stercoris*, is mentioned in the Domesday book as being in use at Chester.

Devil's Mark

All accused were subjected to a search for evidence of a Devil's mark – witch hunters believed the Devil always made a permanent mark on the body of his initiates to seal their pact. This was accomplished by raking his claw across their flesh or using a hot iron, supposedly at the end of the initiation rites which were performed on the night of Sabbats (one of eight major seasonal festivals): leaving a mark, usually blue or red, but not a scar.

The marks were made in secret places on the body, such as in armpits, under the eyelids and in body cavities. Scars, birthmarks, natural blemishes and insensitive patches of skin were often taken as being the Devil's mark, although witch-hunters believed the mark to be clearly distinguishable from other blemishes.

If no mark could be found the accused was searched for invisible marks by the process of pricking. It seems if the accusers wanted to find a mark they would go to all lengths to find one.

Ducking Stool

The accused would have been strapped to a wooden chair fastened to a long beam by a rope or chain that could be swung out across the river or pond, and using a see-saw like motion the person would be dunked. The ducking stool was not usually fixed and would have been mounted on wheels so it could be wheeled through the streets. It was often used as a common scold (punishment) with magistrates deciding how many duckings the guilty person received. The ducking could last from just seconds upwards and it was not unknown for 'accidental' deaths to occur. Ducking stools were still known to be in use as late as the nineteenth century.

On the 30 June 1735 John Kinsman, a shoemaker from Naseby, was, according to the *Northampton Mercury*, 'conducted to a great pond in Kelmarsh Lordship, and underwent the discipline of the ducking stool for being suspected as a wizard, and conspiring with the Devil, his master, to prevent the lazy dairy woman's good butter and cheese, &c'. Upwards of 1,000 spectators were present. One of the spectators, a Mister Barwick, also got into the water claiming he would sink before the wizard. But, unfortunately for the hopeful crowd, he didn't, and the accused sank and was therefore freed.

Miscellaneous Poems, written by Benjamin West and published in 1780, includes a poem entitled *The Ducking stool*:

There stands, my friend, in yonder pool
An engine called the ducking-stool;
By legal power commanded down
The joy and terror of the town.
If jarring females kindle strife,
Give language foul, or lug the coif,
If noisy dames should once begin
To drive the house with horrid din,
Away, you cry, you'll grace the stool;
We'll teach you how your tongue to rule.
The fair offender fills the seat
In sullen pomp, profoundly great;
Down in the deep the stool descends,
But here, at first, we miss our ends;
She mounts again and rages more
Than ever vixen did before.
So, throwing water on the fire
Will make it but burn up the higher.
If so, my friend, pray let her take
A second turn into the lake,
And, rather than your patience lose,
Thrice and again repeat the dose.
No brawling wives, no furious wenches,
No fire so hot but water quenches.

Pricking

This was a common method used in the sixteenth and seventeenth centuries to discover if the accused was indeed a witch. If no Devil's mark could be found it was conveniently decided by the investigators that the Devil sometimes made a small area of the body of the witch insensitive

Seventeenth-century woodcut of the ducking stool.

A ducking stool.

to pain or that would not bleed when pricked. Needles, pins or bodkins would be jabbed into the skin all over the body. Although the discovery of such an area was rarely enough to convict the accused it would work as evidence against them in the upcoming trial. England employed professional witch-finders and they often earned their fees on the amount of witches they found, so it was not uncommon that tricks were used during the pricking process, i.e. fake bodkins.

Shaving and Probing

Once imprisoned the accused was first asked to confess. Sometimes the mere thought of the torture to come was enough to raise a confession, but if this did not raise the desired effect the first course of action would be shaving and probing. The victim would be stripped naked and shaved, in the hope of causing embarrassment and humiliation. In the case of women it was not uncommon to have this procedure done by a man. Shaving was also done to stop the Devil hiding in their body hair and aiding them in the upcoming trial. They would be probed all over too, in case they were hiding any magical charms in their orifices.

Swimming

Henry III declared the swimming test illegal in 1219, however, it was still used by mobs of villagers who conducted their own unofficial tests, and in some cases the courts regarded swimming as a valuable first step in the trial process and happily turned a blind eye. The trial by water consisted of binding the hands and feet of the accused, usually the right thumb to the right toe or 'cross bound', right thumb to left toe, and then being plunged into a river, lake or pond. Proof or guilt was decided on whether they sank or swam, it was generally believed that if they floated they were guilty as the Devil helped them survive. The problem with this method was that innocent people who sank and passed the test often drowned before they were pulled out of the water.

King James I endorsed trial by swimming stating in his book *Daemonologie* (1597) that, 'God hath appointed (for a supernatural signe of the monstrous impietie of Witches) that the water shall refuse to receive them in her bosome, that have shaken off them the sacred Water of Baptisme, and willfully refused the benefit thereof.' James was convinced witchcraft was rife in his kingdom and believed that baptized Christians who were in league with the Devil would float.

As the mobs craved excitement, accidental deaths like that of Ruth Osborne caused the government to threaten death by hanging to the offenders, but this did not stop many people being rounded up and dunked regardless. On 1 August 1785, the *Northampton Mercury* recorded:

> that on Thursday last a poor woman, named Sarah Bradshaw, of Mears Ashby, in this county, who was accused by some of her neighbours of being a witch, in order to prove her innocence, submitted to the ignominy of being dipped, when she immediately sunk to the bottom of the pond, which was deemed an incontestable proof that she was no witch!

Another strange case occurred in the early 1800s involving an old woman named Walden or Warden from St John Street, Wellingborough. She unfortunately had the reputation of being a witch, and was taken by a large crowd to a place called Warren's Mill. She was thrown in but began to swim. After floating there for a while her son William, having heard of her abduction, appeared and was heard to say, 'witch or Devil, she's my mother, and I'll have her,' and then it appears he dived in and saved her. She went onto live a few more years but this didn't stop the locals from judging her a witch.

Watching or Waking

Painful physical torture was more isolated in England, with 'induced torture' preferred. One of the most common methods employed was watching or waking. This involved depriving the

The 'swimming' of Mary Sutton, a woodcut from 1615.

victim of sleep until a hallucinatory state set in forcing the victim's spirit to be broken and a confession usually followed. Ways to keep the victim awake included chaining them to a wall using a very short chain, with an iron bridle placed on the head – making it impossible for the accused to sit or lie down – as well as forcing them to sit cross-legged on a small stool.

Walking

This was reputedly Matthew Hopkins' preferred method of gaining a confession. Again this was an 'induced torture', where the victim was walked back and forth to the point of absolute exhaustion. Although walking does not sound that unpleasant, the process could last for days at a time, and usually produced the desired effect.

WITCH BALLS

Decorative glass balls roughly seven inches in diameter, usually blue or green in colour, were hung in windows throughout England in the eighteenth century as a way of warding off witches' spells and general ill fortune. Some witch balls were made of reflective glass to act as mirrors and were used for decorative purposes as well.

WITCH BOTTLES

Glass, iron and Bellarmine jars were used as witch bottles. They would be filled with the victim's urine, nail clippings and sometimes strands of hair. Once this was done there were many ways to use the bottle for protection. It could be buried under the hearth of the fire causing the spell to be broken as well as inflicting great pain and discomfort on the person who cast the spell. Another method was to boil the bottle on the hearth; this again caused great pain to the caster causing him or her to lift the spell, or it was thought that it caused the witch to be drawn to the boiling liquid therefore exposing their identity. The final method involving fire was that the bottle could be sealed and placed in a fire until it exploded, the explosion breaking the spell and killing the witch. As well as these uses mentioned it was not uncommon to hang a bottle in the chimney as a charm to prevent witches flying down the chimney. It is thought that the procedure for making an effective witch bottle was quite a process, and sources suggest while the urine was warmed the Lord's Prayer was recited over and over, giving the bottle the power to break the spell and reverse it.

Witch bottles were mostly used throughout East Anglia, where belief in witchcraft and superstition were strongest, although it is said they were introduced from Holland. Bellarmine jars were stone wine or beer bottles imported from along the Rhine River near Cologne, Germany, featuring the face of Cardinal Bellarmino (1542-1621), one of the leaders of the Counter Reformation. They were also called Beardman jugs due to their appearance – they often have heraldic decorations and the coats of arms of European cities. The coats of arms appearing on the jar referred to the city for which they were intended for export. They date back to the seventeenth and early eighteenth centuries. Bellarmines were copied in England around 1675 by John Dwight of Fulham.

The Northampton Museum and Art Gallery has a stock of these old bottles, some donated in the nineteenth century and others excavated in local buildings. These bottles, now cleaned, have not been tested for urine but similar Bellarmine witch bottles have been found in Lincolnshire recently.

WITCH BOXES

Witch boxes were another form of charm used in protection against witchcraft throughout Britain. They were very popular in the sixteenth and seventeenth centuries and were usually a small wooden box, sometimes glass fronted, filled with herbs, rowan twigs, pieces of bone and general odds and ends. A spell of protection would be cast over the box to save the occupants of the house from witches' spells and to prevent them from entering the home. These boxes would often have been sold by witch-hunters who travelled around Britain at this time raising the public's interest in witches.

WITCH DOLLS OR EFFIGIES

The use of an effigy formed in the likeness of a person who witches wished to harm was apparently very common in witchcraft, and evidence has been found of the practice dating back to ancient Egypt. The effigy would be made of wax or lead, as well as other materials such as clay and wood.

It was widely believed that if a witch caused damage to the effigy then a similar fate would affect to person the doll represented. Often the doll would contain hair, nail clippings or a piece of clothing of the intended victim which would then be stuck with pins, thorns or nails, causing considerable pain to the corresponding limb. Another method was to burn or melt the effigy.

Bellarmine jar found at site of the Boot Inn, College Street. (Courtesy Northampton Central Museum)

Bellarmine jar found at Leadenhall Market. (Courtesy Northampton Central Museum)

Bellarmine jar
found at the site
of the Old Police
Station, Dychurch
Lane. (Courtesy
Northampton Central
Museum)

WITCHING HOUR

The witching hour occurs at midnight on the night of the fool's moon, when the witch's powers are at their height. The belief in the witching hour dates back to ancient times and the worship of goddesses associated with the moon and fertility. As the moon waxes and wanes through its cycle so do the powers relating to its deities, until the witches' powers regain full strength at the next full moon.

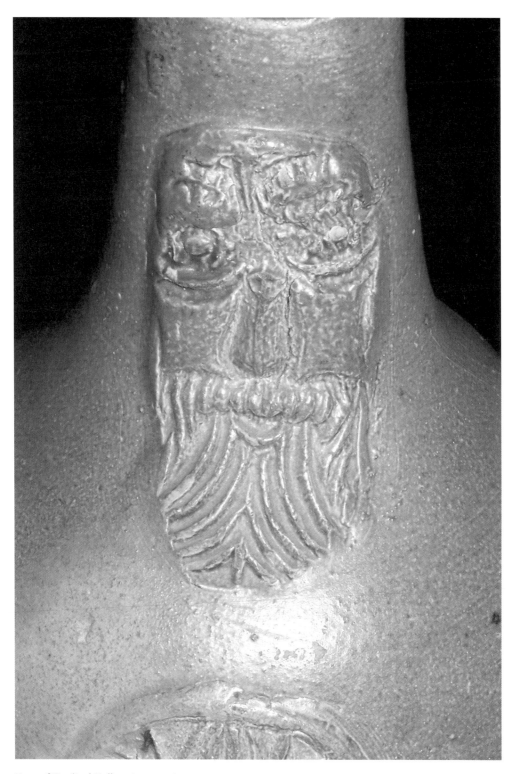

Face of Cardinal Bellarmino on a jar.

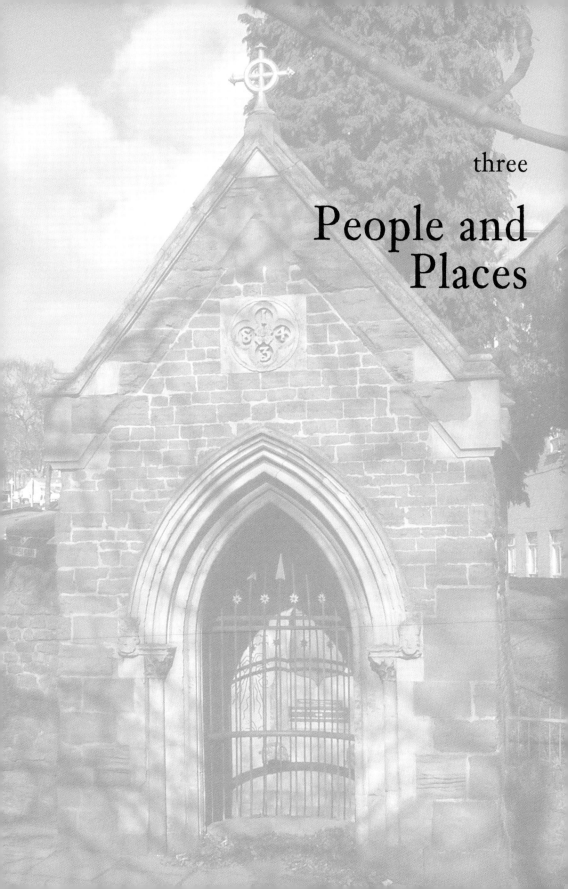

three

People and
Places

John Norden in his travels of the country in 1590 says of Northamptonshire:

> This Towne is a fayre Towne with many fayre old buildings lardge streets and a very ample fayre market Place. It is walled about with a wall of stone but meane of strength, neare unto the Towne theare standeth an auncient castel ruynous.

NORTHAMPTON CASTLE

There was a castle in Northampton from the beginning of the eleventh century, originally built by Simon de St Liz or Senlis, the first Norman Earl of Northampton. He was also responsible for the founding of the priory of St Andrew, around 1094, and the rebuilding of most of the town, which was partly ruinous at the time of his arrival. He had also built the church of the Holy Sepulchre as a thank you for his safe return from the first Crusade, but he wasn't so lucky in the second and was killed on his way back, being buried in France. His widow Matilda married the Prince of Scotland, and the earldom passed into his hands for a short while; it was generally thought that the castle passed into royal hands in 1173, but an entry in the Pipe Rolls of 1131 clearly shows that Northampton Castle was already regarded as royal property by 1130. It was in this castle that the first 'witchcraft' trial took place.

Printed in *Northamptonshire Notes and Queries* and Taylor & Son's pamphlet *1866* is the case of Thomas à Becket, who, it was said, was charged with sorcery by Henry II at Northampton Castle in 1164. The truth behind this though it seems is more to do with religion than sorcery. Thomas was born around 1118 in Cheapside, London to Matilda and Gilbert Beket, both Normans possibly from La Bec, France. He was educated in England and then France, returning home aged twenty-one after his mother's death. He found employment as a banker's clerk in London, later moving on to work for the Theobald, Archbishop of Canterbury.

King Henry II sent for Thomas in 1154 to become his new royal chancellor, and during this time he led an army in France. Despite the age gap of fourteen years Thomas and Henry became firm friends, constantly spending their time together either at work or hunting in their free time. Theobald died in 1161 and was replaced by Thomas the following year, the only problem being that Thomas had never been ordained. This was quickly solved however, when Thomas was invested first as a priest, then the following day ordained as a bishop and that same afternoon (2 June 1162), made Archbishop of Canterbury.

The post of archbishop changed Thomas. He abandoned the luxuries he was used to, preferring to eat bread and drink water and follow a strict religious life. Signs of a split between Thomas and Henry began to show. In 1163, a canon accused of murder was acquitted by a Church court. A public outcry demanded justice, and the canon was brought before a court of the King. Thomas protested and this put a halt to the trial. The following year a furious Henry called a royal council meeting at his hunting lodge at Clarendon. Here, the Constitutions of Clarendon were drawn up, under which the Church maintained the right to try members of the clergy, but if they were found guilty they were then sent to the royal courts for sentence. Thomas agreed to accept the ruling at first but later changed his mind and refused to sign the order.

This stand prompted a royal summons to Henry's court at Northampton Castle on 8 October, where a great Council of Barons was held and the archbishop cited to appear. Thomas was treated as a criminal throughout rather than as someone of his social standing. While the trial was in progress, a matter of five days, Henry remained in the castle while Thomas stayed at the priory of St Andrew. Thomas was first charged with failing to do justice in the case of John the Marshal, for which he was fined £500 and he was also asked to account for money which had passed through his hands while chancellor. On Tuesday 13 October he returned to St Andrew's to celebrate the Mass of St Stephen, with the Eucharist '*Etenim sederunt principles*' (Princes have sat and spoken against me). He then went back to the castle and, holding aloft his cross, entered the Great Hall. News of his entrance reached Henry, who viewed it as an 'unpardonable insult to the crown'.

When the bishops reported what Thomas had done at Mass, and also that he had appealed to Rome, Henry was even more irate. He sent down an ultimatum – withdraw the appeal to Rome and submit to the King's Court regarding the accounts. Thomas refused and committed himself to the protection of God and the Pope. He was charged with contempt of royal authority and malfeasance (from the Latin *malefacere*, 'to do evil'). It is this charge that more than likely led to the assumption that sorcery was involved.

Thomas à Becket denied that the King and his assembly could judge him, saying, 'Do ye pretend to judge me? Ye are but laymen. I am your spiritual father and I refuse to listen to you'. Feeling his life was too valuable to the Church he decided to escape while he could, so cross in hand he walked across the crowded hall – all the while being hailed with shouts of 'traitor, traitor'. Stopping long enough in the courtyard to mount his horse (and to pick up his 'faithful Herbert of Bosham', who had lost his horse amongst the crowd) he was quickly outside the castle gates, to the delight of the crowds who were kneeling to receive his blessing as he passed by on his way to the monastery of St Andrew. Once there he invited some of the poorer people to share his supper, before retiring to his bed in the monastic church. The monks sang their midnight matins very quietly, fearing that they would disturb their guest, but there was really no need because in the dead of night, in a torrent of rain, Thomas had slipped out of the North Gate of the town and was well on his way before anyone discovered he was gone.

It is strongly believed that on his escape he stopped at a spring in Derngate, Northampton for refreshment. In 1843 the local council built a stone structure around the spring, turning it in to what we now know as Becket's Well.

Thomas fled from England to France on 2 November 1164 and remained in exile for six years, living as a monk with the full support of the French King. He sent out numerous letters complaining about Henry until finally the Pope stepped in and threatened him with an interdict (an ecclesiastical or legal sanction), forcing him to end his quarrel with Thomas. A meeting was

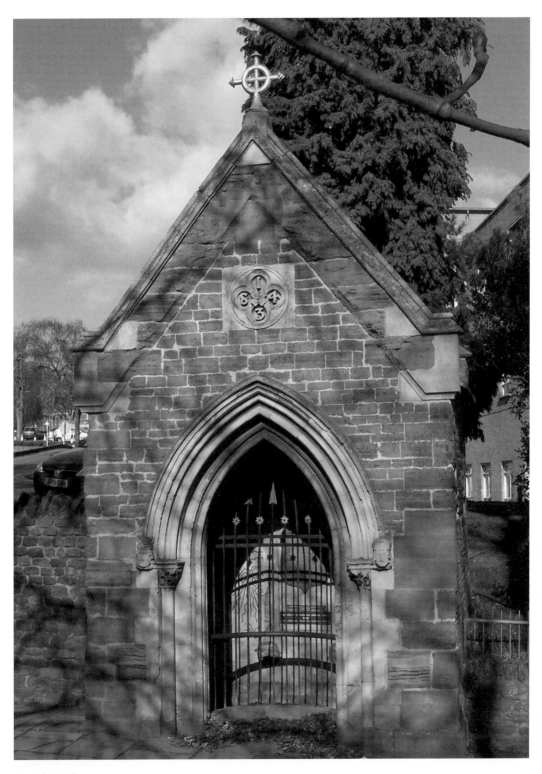

Beckett's Well.

arranged in July 1170 at which it was agreed that Thomas should return as long as he took no action against those who had opposed him in the past.

On his return to England, Thomas immediately excommunicated three priests who had sided with the King in his absence. Henry became furious and has been quoted as saying: 'will no one rid me of this troublesome priest?' Four knights, Reginald FitzUrse, William de Tracey, Hugh de Morville and Richard le Breton, hearing this and hoping to please the King, rode to Canterbury. On 29 December the knights entered Canterbury Cathedral and killed Thomas. It is believed that Thomas's body was lying on the floor when local townsfolk came to the church; they tore pieces of his clothes and dipped them in his blood in the hope they would bring luck and keep away evil. The Pope declared Thomas à Becket a saint in 1173.

The Assize of Northampton came into being in 1176 and was the first of its kind, being based on the Assize of Clarendon of 1166 which was one of a series of measures that King Henry II introduced in an effort to bring royal law and order to the land. A selected council of people sat in judgement, with a pair of judges covering the proceedings, assize being Norman French 'for the gathering together of important people for the purposes of law making'. The assize judges mainly dealt with the more serious offences like murder, rape, highway robbery, recusancy (either refusing to submit to authority or Roman Catholics who refused to attend the services of the Church of England as was required by law) and witchcraft, leaving the petty criminals to be dealt with by the Sessions Courts. The assizes were generally held twice a year, summer and winter, and carried right through to the middle of the twentieth century. There are assize rolls still in existence dating back to the thirteenth century. In 1971 they were abolished and replaced by the Crown Courts.

The castle also housed the town gaol. As well as keeping the criminal element incarcerated, it also had as its 'guest' Sir Justinian Isham, who in 1658 was imprisoned with other Royalists at the request of Oliver Cromwell. Sir Justinian, in a letter he wrote, said that most of them suffered from 'extreme colds'. It was Sir Justinian himself who had a hand in the demolition of the castle after the Restoration when in 1662, following an order from the King and council, much of the castle, walls and gates came down. The site was afterwards sold for £50 to a gentleman of the town; it remained in his possession until the middle of the nineteenth century, when it was sold to the London & North Western Railway Company, apparently for £15,000.

The castle had been patronized by many Kings over the centuries and put to a variety of uses; in 1131 it was the seat of the National Parliament, the twelfth century saw the first assizes to be held at the castle and in 1189 Northampton was given permission by King John to select a reeve (mayor) for the first time. In 1215, William Tilly became the first mayor of Northampton. In 1215, civil war broke out, the barons having fallen out with John over the money he was squeezing out of them to pay for his army (and his personal use) and because he began depriving them of their estates. The barons laid siege to the castle for fourteen days, causing much damage to the town and castle while King John hid inside. John managed a truce but this ultimately led to the signing of the Magna Carta, in which John promised that the barons would be designated Northampton Castle plus three others as securities against his promises. However, John managed to hold on to everything and continue arguing with the barons right up until his death in 1216. By 1338 the castle was falling into disrepair and by 1380 was in quite a dangerous state, although it was still used as a court house, prison and government offices. Parliament met here for the first time in 1380.

Northampton was no stranger to destruction though – a fire in 1516 destroyed much of the town, another fire in 1566 destroyed a bit more, and finally the great fire of Northampton in 1675 managed to take out three quarters of the town. According to *Northampton Past and Present*, 'a handy guide book' *c.* 1890, the course of the fortifications of the town was still visible up until the middle

Postern Gate.

THIS POSTERN GATE OR SIDE ENTRANCE IS ALL THAT REMAINS OF A ONCE IMPRESSIVE ROYAL RESIDENCE, NORTHAMPTON CASTLE. MEDIEVAL KINGS HELD PARLIAMENTS HERE. IN 1164 THE TRIAL OF THOMAS BECKET, ARCHBISHOP OF CANTERBURY TOOK PLACE IN THE CASTLE. AFTER THE CIVIL WAR IT WAS MADE UNINHABITABLE ON THE ORDERS OF CHARLES II. FOLLOWING CENTURIES OF NEGLECT THE SITE WAS CLEARED IN 1879 TO MAKE WAY FOR NORTHAMPTON RAILWAY STATION. THE POSTERN GATE WAS DISMANTLED AND REBUILT HERE IN THE EARLY 1880s AS A MONUMENT TO THE CASTLE.

Northamptonshire County Council · Network SouthEast · Northampton Borough Council

1993

Postern Gate Sign.

of the nineteenth century and was traceable around Derngate, St Giles' church, St Edmund's, along the Mounts, St Sepulchre and St Andrews Mill, where part of the fosse still remained, but, 'These traces have however been swept away by the relentless hand of modern growth and improvement.' Northampton Castle has all but disappeared now, apart from a few remains, with nothing much to show for its long and distinguished career except maybe Northampton Castle Railway station, which opened right on top of the site of the original castle!

NORTHAMPTON GAOL

Originally most people who went to gaol did so because they were in debt. The prison was supported by voluntary contributions and as a consequence was often in a state of disrepair and escapes were all too frequent. A watch was posted to try and combat this problem. With more and more people arriving in gaol for all sorts of nefarious reasons it was decided to split the debtors' gaol from the criminal one. After moving from the castle in 1662 the gaol (although there is very little evidence for this) is believed to have been moved to the Guildhall, where part of the present Northampton Museum is today. There is, however, a small piece written in a book entitled *A Brief Account of the Sufferings of the Quakers*, published in 1690, that describes the case of seven people who were imprisoned in the 'Low Gaol' for not paying their tithes, all unfortunately dying within

A view of the remaining castle monuments.

a few months of being imprisoned. Apparently this Low Gaol was a dungeon, 'twelve steps below ground,' with up to thirty men in it at any one time, 'and in the night they had little air, being lockt down betimes, and so kept close until the seventh hour the next morning'. It recorded that the wife of one of the prisoners 'died from a pestiferous disease contracted in this loathsome place'.

In the nineteenth century two new gaols were built separating the borough from the county. The Borough Gaol and House of Correction was built at Upper Mounts at a cost of £17,000. In the late 1800s it was changed to Her Majesty's Prison after the government purchased it for £1,950 under the Prisons Act of 1898 which made sweeping changes to the prison system with the outlawing of the crank and treadwheel and changes to prison labour. The Borough Gaol stayed on the Mounts until 1922 and was demolished in 1931; it is now the site of the Mounts Swimming Baths, the fire station and Campbell Square police station. The County Gaol in Angel Lane cost £25,000 and was bigger but with smaller cells. In 1858 a new county police station opened in Dychurch Lane complete with fire engine and stabling for the horses, it seems the policemen doubled up as firemen too!

THE GALLOWS

Originally gallows were set up wherever they happened to be needed, but over time it was decided that a permanent structure would be better to deal with all hangings from around the county. The first recorded gallows were set up in Abington Village, just a couple of miles north-east of Northampton and it was here that the witches of 1612 met their death. Although these

NORTHAMPTON CASTLE WAS PROBABLY FIRST BUILT IN THE LATE 11th CENTURY, PERHAPS AS A SIMPLE EARTH AND TIMBER MOTTE AND BAILEY. IT WAS CONSIDERABLY STRENGTHENED DURING THE NEXT 200 YEARS WHEN IT GREW TO NATIONAL IMPORTANCE, BUT WAS IN DECLINE BY THE 14th CENTURY AND 'SLIGHTED' BY CHARLES II AFTER THE CIVIL WAR. IT WAS THE SCENE OF THOMAS A BECKET'S TRIAL BEFORE KING HENRY II (1164) AND WAS MUCH FREQUENTED BY KING JOHN.
THE PLAN SHOWS WALLS RECORDED IN 1863 AND OTHERS UNCOVERED IN 1961-4. BUILDINGS WERE GROUPED AROUND THE OUTSIDE OF THE INNER BAILEY. THE MAIN GATEWAY WAS TO THE NORTH, AND AN OUTER BAILEY LAY TO THE SOUTH.

Castle monument sign.

gallows were meant to deal with all the hangings for Northamptonshire there were recorded instances where convicted criminals of particularly nasty and obnoxious crimes would be hanged as near to the scene of their crime as possible. The gallows remained at Abington until at least 1638, when the record states that Arthur Bett was hanged here. The next hanging took place in 1651, when Leonard Bland was hanged, 'on new gallows made for him'. These were situated near Northampton Heath and remained here for the next 100 years. The advent of Northampton's field enclosure in 1779, however, made it improper that the gallows should be on any one person's private allotment of land, so the decision was taken for the gallows to be moved. They were re-erected on the corner of the Racecourse, which today is on the opposite side of the road to the White Elephant public house. They remained here until 1818, when the authorities felt that they should be removed due to the large and unruly crowds that congregated every time someone was transported from the gaol and through the streets of Northampton to the Racecourse. The solution was to have the new gallows situated at the rear of the County Gaol in Angel Lane. This again was a permanent fixture, but so the crowds could get a good view from Cow Meadow they were placed high up. Instead of having the back of a cart suddenly pull out from under them, the condemned stood on a trapdoor, which resulted in the new gallows becoming known as the 'new drop.' For fifty years it remained there until 1868, when a Prison Act made public executions illegal and the gallows were moved inside the prison walls.

The people responsible for the trials were the High Sheriffs and his Majesty's Justices of the Peace – let us encounter a few of them.

Site of the old Abington Gallows.

SIR THOMAS TRESHAM

In 1607, during a particularly troublesome time in the county (during the Midland Riot against enclosure), Sir Thomas was out riding one evening with a couple of friends, Sir Anthony Mildmay and Sir Robert Montacute, when they noticed at least 1,000 men digging with staves and bill-hooks near Thomas's home village of Newton. Not seeing the situation clearly, they thought they were up against men armed with pykes, bows and arrows and thinking they were rebels, Sir Thomas demanded to see the leader who was told that the man in charge was called 'Captain Pouch'. Finally, the captain stood in front of Sir Thomas, who asked for his name and was told it was John Reynolds. Sir Thomas asked him why, if his name was John Reynolds, his men called him 'Captain Pouch'. Mr Reynolds explained that the reason was because he carried a pouch around with him which contained both 'magic and divine inspiration', which gave him the right to lead his people. A furious Sir Thomas ordered for him to be seized and searched and having ripped his pouch from him they opened it to find it contained '…a piece of green cheese!'

Sir Thomas Tresham of Newton was also related to Francis Tresham of Gunpowder Plot fame.

SIR THOMAS BROOKE OF OAKLEY

The Brooke family had been at Great Oakley since the fifteenth century, and had always taken a prominent part in local affairs whether as magistrates, deputy lieutenants or even a High Sheriff or two. Thomas's father Arthur Brooke was Master of the Hart Hounds to Queen Elizabeth I. They had links with many of the old-established names throughout the county through various marriages, including John Brooke , Thomas's ancestor who married Isabel, the daughter of Thomas Wake of Blisworth. Other family names included the Watsons of Rockingham, Montagus of Broughton and the Ishams of Lamport.

During the Civil War in 1650 Sir Thomas Brooke, in his capacity as Justice of the Peace, was instructed to search Rockingham Castle, the home of Sir Lewis Watson, who was under suspicion by the Council of State. He did this, but first he sent a letter to Sir Lewis saying:

> being my duty to be faithful to the state yet desirous to shew myselfe civill to your lordship: I have sent an officer in whom I repose trust to put in execution that said order from whom you shall receive that civill respect as if I were present, and therefore desire that he may search without disturbance that I may faithfully perform the trust imposed upon me

He ended the letter with, 'your Lordshipp's affectionate cousin and servant, Thos Brooke'.

SIR GILBERT PICKERING OF TITCHMARSH

Sir Gilbert was another gentleman who was very well-connected to various families around the county. His son John married one of Sir Erasmus Dryden's daughters, and his niece Mary Pickering married Erasmus Dryden, Sir Erasmus's third son, and was the mother John Dryden, one of Northamptonshire's most famous poets. Sir Gilbert was also connected to the Throckmorton family of Croughton by the marriage of his sister Elizabeth to Robert Throckmorton Esq., lord of the manor of Ellington, which led to him becoming involved in a tale of witchcraft that centred on the village of Warboys. This was home to Mr and Mrs Throckmorton and their five children, who ranged in age from six to fifteen. Robert Throckmorton was also related to the Treshams of Rushton and the Catesbys, through his second cousin Muriel Throckmorton who married Sir Thomas Tresham, 'The Builder' (1543-1605). Both Francis Tresham and Robert Catesby were implicated in the Gunpowder Plot.

At the end of 1589 Jane (aged ten), one of Robert Throckmortons' daughters, was seized with fits to such a degree that she had to be tied down to the bed. Thinking that his daughter was suffering from some sort of 'palsy', Robert called for a doctor. Having made his examination, the doctor determined that this was not a case of palsy at all but more likely a case of witchcraft. An elderly neighbour, Mrs Alice Samuel, as was the custom of the time, came to visit the Throckmortons to enquire as to the health of young Jane; it was whilst she was sitting by the fireside that Jane, in-between fits, cried out, 'look at where the old witch sits. Did you ever see anyone more like a witch than she is.....I cannot bear to look at her'. Shortly afterwards Alice left the house, not knowing that this persecution would go on for a couple of years.

It was not long after this that another – and then another – child became similarly afflicted and before the New Year had begun all five were suffering from fits. Whilst they were in such a state they regularly called out the name of Mother Samuel, crying that she had bewitched them. Sir Gilbert, upon hearing what was happening to his sister's children, decided to visit them.

When he arrived on the 13 February Mother Samuel had just been sent for, but she refused to come. It is believed that she was afraid of being 'scratched'. Sir Gilbert then took it upon himself to go to Mother Samuel's house to see if he could persuade her to come and see the children, and, if indeed she was the cause of their problems, put them right. He apparently had to use some threats to get her to agree, but she finally consented and, taking her daughter Agnes with her, made her way to the Throckmorton house.

When she arrived, three of the children were by the fireside showing no untoward symptoms at all, but as soon as Mrs Samuel and Agnes entered the room they fell down, 'strangely tormented, so that, if they had been let alone, they would have leaped and sprung about like a fish newly taken out of the water.' Sir Gilbert thought it would be a good idea to take one of the children home with him to see if it made any difference, but to no avail – she continued to have convulsions.

Lady Cromwell (the grandmother of Oliver Cromwell) also visited the family, and decided to have a talk with Alice. It is alleged that Alice said, 'why are you afraid of me for I have never harmed you yet?' It is also alleged that Lady Cromwell:

call'd her a witch, and abused her, and pulled off her kerchief, and cut off some of her hair, and gave it to Mrs Throckmorton for a charm. At night this lady, as was very likely she would after such an ill day's work, dreamt of Mother Samuel and a cat, and fell into fits.

Lady Cromwell never regained complete health and died about fifteen months later. Her death was also attributed to the witchcraft practices of Alice Samuel. Meanwhile, Robert Throckmortons' children were all still suffering from convulsions, and were observed to mutter stories about imps belonging to Alice, especially Jane who reported long conversations between the imps to Dr Dorrington. According to one record, these were called Pluck, Smack, Hardname, Catch and Blew. This continued right up to the Christmas of 1592, when the stress of the situation got too much for poor Alice and she confessed to the priest that she was indeed a witch. When Mr Samuel and Agnes heard what she had done they begged her to change her mind and recant, knowing that she was no witch, but it was too late – Alice Samuel was taken into custody along with her husband and daughter, for by siding with Alice they had made themselves suspects too.

During the trial on 4 April 1593 at the Court Hall, Huntingdon, Cambridgeshire, at least 500 people turned up to watch the proceedings. They witnessed the Throckmorton children having fits and heard Alice admit that she was a witch and did indeed cause the death of Lady Cromwell, and heard her say, 'I charge the Devil to suffer Mistress Jane to come out of her fit'. Initially John Samuel refused to say anything, but the threat of immediate execution by Judge Jenner made him change his mind. After the Samuels had made their oaths, all the Throckmorton children apparently became well again, but it was too late for Alice, John and Agnes, they were found to be guilty and two days later were hanged at Mill Common.

The Samuel property was sold off and the £40 that was made from it was given to Sir Henry Cromwell, husband of Lady Cromwell, 'which he bequeathed for a sermon to be preached on the evils of witchcraft every Lady Day [25 March] in Huntingdon by a Doctor of Divinity from Cambridge'. The sermon would, 'Invaye againste the detestable practice synne and offence of witchcraft'. It is believed that this sermon was preached in All Saints church, Huntingdon, right up until 1814.

Sir Gilbert had a bit of a reputation as a witch-finder and was also involved in the Gunpowder Plot … searching out the conspirators!

Titchmarsh church, the burial place of Sir Gilbert Pickering.

THE ISHAMS OF LAMPORT

The Ishams are one of Northamptonshire's oldest families, also very well respected and well connected. During the War of the Roses, the Ishams of Pytchley were very much in favour of the House of York and when King Edward married his Northamptonshire bride the family status rose quite quickly. Robert Isham of Pytchley was Elizabeth Woodville's solicitor general as well as controller of the great custom in the Port of London. (Sir John's sister-in-law Anne was married to Sir Lawrence Washington of Garsden, who was a grandson of the Washington's of Sulgrave – there is a letter from Anne to her sister Judith, Sir John's wife, which has the Washington seal on it, stars and stripes…).

They had land around Isham (the origin of the name) from before the Conquest. John Isham, Sir John's grandfather, moved to Lamport in 1560. John Isham was High Sheriff of the county in 1581, a profession his grandson, Sir John Isham, also pursued. Sir John was a big record keeper and a lot of his papers, including the ones from his time as High Sheriff, are kept at the Northampton Record Office. Sir John took a considerable part in local affairs and was knighted by King James. King Charles I gave him the baronetcy in 1627. In later years he became impoverished by his loans to the King (whom he supported) and by 'fines imposed by Parliament'.

Sir John died in 1651 and in order that the Prayer Book Service could be conducted (it was forbidden at that time), he was buried quietly at midnight. Sir John was succeeded by his son Justinian, whose support for the Royalists led him to be imprisoned at Northampton Castle. After the Restoration Sir Justinian became a Member of Parliament for the county; he also became a baronet, a title which his son Thomas inherited in 1675. It was Thomas Isham who kept a diary at his father's request from 1671 to 1673, being paid £6 to do so on the proviso that he wrote it in Latin. It is from this translated diary that we get a little tale of witchcraft from Great Bowden in 1673.

It started on the 1 February. One of the Ishams' servants, having heard about some witches in Bowden, asked Sir Justinian for permission to go to see for himself what was going on. Sir Justinian agreed. Upon his return he told his tale: a hard-working, reasonably wealthy weaver had gone to Market Harborough to buy some food stuffs while his wife and children stayed at home. After a little while the mother asked her children if they could go and meet him and help him with the shopping, but just before they left a woman came up and said that she'd like to go with them. The mother wasn't too happy about this because she had heard various stories about this woman – including one about a man who was on his deathbed and accusing her of putting him there. Eventually the mother let them go.

On the way they met a man who nodded his head at them. The woman said: 'Are you nodding at me, you impudent rogue? I'll send cats to haunt you.' This upset the eldest girl and not long after she became bewitched, as did all the other children. After William Branson the carrier, who was himself from Great Bowden, related all this to Sir Justinian, for some reason he asked them to have a look at the pillows. When they did this, they found that the feathers inside were stuck together in a particular fashion, so they burned them on the fire. The children who were bewitched made noises like cats and dogs and while in fits constantly called the name of Mrs Brown, one of the local women suspected of witchcraft.

The next entry is from the 9 February, in which Thomas makes a note about a letter that a Mr Templer had sent to Sir Justinian explaining that he didn't believe it was witchcraft and that he was most insulted because, after having successfully treated the eldest daughter, the weaver had seen fit to take her somewhere else and when she returned, she was as bad as before.

The letter, which was dated 1 February, explains that Mr John Templer had been sent to treat the eldest girl, which he did; he had reported his findings about the children back to Sir Justinian

Isham family crest from Lamport Hall.

Lamport Hall, home of the Isham family.

but had asked for more time and information on which to base his diagnosis, mainly because some new evidence had come to light – including the information that he'd just been given by a Madame Francis Haslerigge, who said that that the eldest daughter '...doth now onely counterfeit her fits'.

This was based on the evidence that, a little while after being treated by Mr Templer, she once again began having fits, but when one Madame Brudenells took a light into the dark room where the girl was, she knocked it out of her hand, and the second time she tried to take a light into the room the girl blew it out.

Mr Broughton, the girls' father, had reported that Mr Templer gave 'physicke' to his daughter but she was still as bad as before, but Mr Templer was reported to say, 'whereas it is sufficiently knowne that she was perfectly free from any fit, twixt eleven of the clocke on Munday and five a clocke the Saturday afternoone following.' Mr Templer, taking all these things into account, along with Madame Haslerigge saying that she, 'could not hold downe her arm, which a man could not command in her former fits,' came to believe that the eldest girl was indeed an impostor. He was made even more certain when he was told that the house in which he had treated Mr Broughton's daughter was a 'Quaker's House'.

The next entries covered a four-week period in which Mr Branson said that he didn't agree with Mr Templer, that the girl had had half a dozen really bad fits before going back home and as a consequence was worse than she was before. Mr Templer apparently wrote to the Royal Society detailing all his findings. Mr Gilbert Clerk also went to see Mr Broughton's children and it was his opinion that they had been treated most shamefully. Mr Branson called again at the beginning of March to say that the eldest girl had seemed to be on the mend after vomiting for four or five days, but unfortunately the fits had returned. A week later they heard that one of the witches had admitted that she had bewitched two of the children and that Mrs Brown had confessed that, with the help of another woman, she had put a spell on the three other children. A next-door neighbour of one of the witches had said that sleep was made almost impossible because of a door creaking all nigh; compelling evidence! Thomas also says, 'One of the women is put in prison and her children left to the parish for support.'

Unfortunately, at this time no record can be found as to what happened to the 'Witches of Great Bowden'. Thomas doesn't mention them again, so maybe they were released without charge?! Although the Royal Society kept many letters, including some belonging to Mr Templer, the one pertaining to this case seems to be no longer in evidence. Although it might seem strange to write to the Royal Society about children making noises like cats and dogs, it has to be remembered that Mr Templer thought the children were faking the fits, and because cases of supposed 'witchcraft' were quite common at this time (and the penalty of being found guilty was ultimately death), many scientific men made detailed studies into these cases and reported their findings. Mr Templer was no exception.

In a final note, in a lecture given by Revd J. Jackson at the Town Hall in Northampton in December 1880, he mentions a letter written in the April of 1678 by Mr Gilbert Clerk to Thomas Isham, who was in Rome at the time, in which, after passing the time of day about the coldness of the weather and the storage of some malt ready for the making of some good ale, he then goes on to mention a case involving the widows of Brixworth:

Ever since All Saints they had been haunted with a evil spirit, whose knockings disturbed their rest. How, they then described, sometimes they felt a heavy weight on their shoulders at night, or heard a rooting like a hog in the bedstraw, or had twitches of their head-clothes or chimes were rung on the pancheons.

As Mr Clerk goes on to say 'Tis an odd story', and one to which he didn't want to commit himself just at this time; again, there is no follow-up reference, so did they carry on being haunted? Did it stop as suddenly as it started? Was someone responsible? We will probably never know…

four

Other Cases
of Trials for
Witchcraft

Although not all these cases occurred within our county's boundaries they are still heavily linked to Northamptonshire and we feel they have to be included for completeness.

IRON AGE WITCH

Although a printed article on witchcraft in Northamptonshire names Thomas à Becket as the first case in the county, the *Northampton Chronicle & Echo* printed a story about what they believed to be evidence of the discovery of England's first witch.

On 11 September 1998 the *Chronicle* reported the discovery of the remains of a woman in a former Iron Age village near Great Houghton. The skeleton carbon dated as being 2,400 years old and was wearing a unique lead collar around her neck, possibly showing she was buried alive. Andrew Selkirk, editor of *Current Archaeology*, was convinced that the woman had been feared for her powers and the heavy collar was put on to keep her symbolically in her grave. He said, 'The only answer which fits the facts is that she was a Celtic witch, buried weighted down to keep her from moving.'

The skeleton was described by Rob Atkins of the Northampton Archaeology Unit as a unique find, as she had been buried in a crouched position with her hands tied with the lead 'torc' around her neck. Gold and silver torcs have been found, but never in this part of the country and never made of lead.

Analysis of the skeleton showed the woman to be of between the ages of thirty and forty years old, with her knees showing a great deal of wear, 'as though she had spent a lot of time kneeling'. He agreed that the witch theory was 'possible', although his colleague Andy Chapman felt the woman had been buried alive as an offering for future fertility after a bad harvest and may have done so willingly.

THE DUCHESS AND THE KING

The *Antiquarian Memoranda XXX* mentions an early case of witchcraft involving royalty, the case of the Duchess of Bedford:

On Tuesday evening, the Revd J. Jackson Goadby, F.G.S. of Henley-on-Thames, delivered the first of a series of lectures on Northamptonshire History and Literature in the Town-Hall at Northampton. Mr Goadby, in his first part of his lecture, dealt at some length, and in a very interesting manner with the general subject. He illustrated the origin and nature of the Superstition, and detailed some of the horrible cruelties that were inflicted on men and women, who were suspected of witchcraft and wizardry. Referring to the subject locally, cited the case of the Dowager Duchess of Bedford, who was declared by an Act of Parliament to be guilty of Sorcery and Witchcraft in securing the hand of King Edward the fourth for her daughter Elizabeth Woodville, widow of Sir John Grey, whose connection with Grafton Regis in this county is well-known.

It was important for the monarchy to make matrimonial alliances; however, for Edward IV his marriage to Elizabeth Woodville was one of pure romance. This would have not been a problem but for the fact that Edward supposedly did not fall in love unassisted and the story goes that the Duchess of Bedford bewitched the King to fall for her daughter.

Edward was well known for his generosity and friendly disposition, much to the embarrassment of his councillors. Apparently while he was on a lone hunting trip in Whittlebury forest he met Elizabeth Woodville under a giant oak tree, later renamed the Queen's Oak. It was said the duchess had planned the 'accidental meeting' and, according to Taylor & Son's *Northamptonshire Handbook*, 'if it were not too grave a slander against such august personages, I should be tempted to say that a very crafty mother, with a very pretty, demure and shy daughter, had set a trap, and caught a very green king.'

The Woodville coat of arms.

Elizabeth Woodville.

For the duchess, seeing her daughter becoming Queen was her main aim, and would see her rise in wealth and power. Elizabeth, thought to be a commoner, was actually born of good stock at Grafton Regis around 1437. Her uncle was a prince of Luxembourg, and on her father's side the family tree could be traced back to the twelfth century and contained Richard de WiDevill, who served eight times as High Sheriff of Northamptonshire during the reign of Edward III. His son John also held this position, and grandson Thomas became lord of Grafton.

Edward and Elizabeth married in secret on 1 May 1464 at the manor house, Grafton Regis. She was crowned as Queen on Whit Sunday 1465. Edward immediately set out to reward the Woodvilles, giving them positions of power and many honours. This upset many of his court and they set about finding a solution to their problems. While the King was at Warwick, Thomas Wake, squire of Blisworth, bought charges against the duchess and presented the King with an, 'image of lede made lyke a man of armes, conteynying the length of a mannes finger, and broken in the myddes, and made fast with wyre', saying it was made by 'the Duchess' to use 'wichcraft and sorsory'.

The King did not feel the witch doll was sufficient evidence, and when it was shown to the duchess she merely enquired as to how such items were made. Thomas Wake went on to say that two other dolls existed (of the King and Queen) and they were being held by John Daunger, parish clerk of Stoke Bruene. Unfortunately for Thomas, when he and Mr Daunger were called before the Bishop of Carlisle Daunger denied this and all charges were dropped.

On Edward's death his brother Richard of Gloucester wanted to claim the throne, and to prove Edward's children had no such claim he revived the accusations against the duchess. His act of settlement stated:

> howe the seid pretensed marriage betwixt the king and Elizabeth Grey [her name after her first marriage] was made of grete peresumtion, without knowing and assent of the lords of this land, and also by sorcerie and wichcraft, committed by the said Elizabeth and her moder Jaquett duchess of Bedford, as the common opinion of the people and publique voice and fame is thorough all this land.

The marriage was finally declared null and void by Parliament in the Act *Titulus Regius*, on the grounds that Edward had previously agreed to marry Lady Eleanor Butler. Edward and Elizabeth's ten children were now declared illegitimate, leaving Richard as the next rightful heir.

Richard was crowned King in 1483. He governed as regent for Edward's son Edward V with the title Lord Protector. He is famous for imprisoning Edward and his brother Richard in the Tower of London before being killed at the Battle of Bosworth Field in 1485. Henry V ascended the throne on the death of Richard and declared his parents' marriage valid and Elizabeth was given the title Queen Dowager.

Edward and Elizabeth feature heavily in the William Shakespeare play *The Life and Death of King Richard III*. In Act III Scene IV, Gloster (Richard), in a conversation with Hastings, says:

> Then be your eyes the witness of their evil:
> Look how I am bewitch'd; behold, mine arm Is,
> like a blasted sapling, wither'd up:
> And this is Edward's wife, that monstrous witch,
> Consorted with that harlot-strumpet Shore,
> That by their witchcraft thus have marked me.
> [The 'harlot-strumpet' Shore was Jane Shore – one of the many mistresses of Edward IV.]

Joane Cradock of Maidwell came before the Northampton Assizes on 28 February 1632 on suspicion of witchcraft. The trial was recorded by Sir John Isham who, as a prominent member of society, kept detailed written accounts on various matters ranging from purveyance (the collection or requisition of provisions for a sovereign) to witchcraft.

The first evidence given before Sir John Isham and Sir Thomas Brooke, both 'his Majesty's Justices of the Peace' for Northamptonshire, came from Nicholas Ward of Maidwell. He explained that two years earlier while he was ploughing his field Joane came over to him and pulled out some of the hair from the horse's side, causing the horse to immediately fall 'amisse', rolling on the floor until it died within the hour. He went onto say that Joane had used witchcraft and that he had told her leave the field or he would be forced to use his whip.

More accusations followed from the villagers of Maidwell, with Elizabeth Litchfield explaining how Richard Dalbie, while travelling to Oxendon on 29 September 1629, met Joane, who asked him if he was going to marry Elizabeth. On answering her yes, she replied, 'she would give him that gift, that hee should never have her, and that she would ridd the Towne of him or else shee would hang for it'. The Isham documents include a note written in the margin of the records stating, 'Because she would have had him to have married her daughter'. Elizabeth goes on to say that Joane had asked him for the stick in his hand and that after he surrendered it to her he had been taken ill. The pain was described as 'tormented very, sore in his head and leggs', which continued until his death some eleven days later.

Joane was accused of a second murder, that of Elizabeth Campion, who had had a flea removed from the right side of her face by the accused, only for her face to swell: she immediately started suffering fits until she died shortly afterwards. Several other witnesses took the stand and spoke of Joane's use of witchcraft. Ellen Robbinson told the tale of her daughter Anne Gunnion, and how she was 'stricken speechless' twice after visits from the accused because she had refused to sell her a loaf of bread and some milk. This was followed by Anne taking the stand herself explaining that Joane had persuaded her to call upon the Devil although she could not remember the exact day.

After receiving all the evidence Lords Isham and Brooke ordered seven women to search the body of Joane Cradock, at which point, 'they say and affirme that they do not find the said Joane Craduck to bee as other women and doe rather think that they found about her in their opinion to bee some witchmark being an inch in length and lookinge verie paile.'

Joane denied all charges, only admitting to advising Ellen Robbinson to go to Market Harborough to obtain the services of a witch to cure her daughter and when asked to explain the witch mark she merely pointed out that, 'she had not any thing more than other women'. The lords reviewed the case and found her innocent.

A second case recorded by Sir John Isham was that of Em Nappon of Scaldwell in August 1628. She was accused of bewitching Elizabeth Sharpe and laming Edward Randell. In this case evidence was given by only five people, with Isabell Randell accusing Em of causing her husband to lose the use of his leg. She explained that Em had offered to cure her husband who had been lame for two to three years, but when she applied an ointment it had caused him great pain and he lost the use of his leg completely. When Edward stopped using the ointment he seemed to regain the use of his legs but when Em found out she told Isabell that in three months time, on Midsummer's Eve, his leg would again become lame. Isabell also gave evidence that Em Nappon had told her that she would be unable to say her prayers in church until, 'she had first caused or wished some evil into Elizabeth Sharpe'. This evidence was backed up by Annis Yorke, who stated that Elizabeth had became ill and had been told by the accused that she would get worse, which she did.

Elizabeth Sharpe told the magistrates that as she was a servant to Edward Palmer, Em Nappon had persuaded her to steal 'sundrie things' from her master, but she had later experienced a guilty conscience and admitted her crimes to her master. She went on to explain that Mrs Nappon had not taken kindly to this and had cursed her, telling her, 'thou hast wronged mee, thou shalt bee tormented as if the Divell was in shee'. Within a fortnight Elizabeth was stricken by a shaking fit, followed by the loss of her voice and eventually the loss of the use of her limbs. This continued for a week before she returned to normal, but this normality was short-lived because she was stricken again with the same symptoms, claiming that she sometimes she went deaf or blind and although the bouts only lasted for between four days and a week they had continued right up to the present day. Even during the trial Elizabeth had two fits, which subsided when in the presence of the accused.

During Em Nappon's defence she confessed to receiving eggs, wool and various other items but added it had been over a year and a half since Elizabeth Sharpe had brought her anything else. She also confessed to cursing Elizabeth but denied bewitching, explaining that it had been more out of temper. On the other account of which she was accused, she denied laming Edward Randall, and when questioned about the 'mark or teat' that had been found on her 'privie parts' during an examination she informed the magistrates that she had had it for about seven or eight years and that it had appeared after the birth of one of her children. Parish records confirm that Em did indeed have a child six or seven years previously.

Magistrates Sir John Isham and Sir Thomas Brook did not feel the evidence was compelling enough and all charges were dropped.

WIDOW STIFF

Much of the information for this story comes from a letter Mr Gilbert Clerk wrote to an acquaintance of his in May 1658. It concerns a tale he first heard related to Sir Justinian Isham by a reverend minister. Sir Justinian had wanted Mr Clerk to go and see for himself but at the time Mr Clerk was unable to. He had all but forgotten about it when another friend who happened to live quite near Welton and was a relative of Moses Cowley (the gentleman concerned in the story) repeated the tale to him. Mr Clerk's friend needed to go to Mr Cowley's house on a matter of business, and finding that he had some time on his hands (and to satisfy his curiosity), Mr Clerk decided to go with him, and so to the story.

About a mile away from Daventry, in a village called Welton, lived the Cowley family. Widow Cowley lived with her daughter Widow Stiff and her two daughters. Next-door-but-one lived another Widow Cowley, sister-in-law to the first, and her son Moses and his wife. Apparently they had 'a good estate in land of their own, and [were] very civil and orderly people'. It was Moses who told how the ten-year-old daughter of Widow Stiff in the space of three days had vomited three gallons of water, and that some time after her elder sister had come running in to say that she had now started to throw up stones and coals. This they had to see, so they went with Miss Stiff back to her house where they counted 500 in total, with some weighing in at a quarter of a pound, 'and were so big, as they had enough to do to get them out of her mouth'. Moses himself said he would have difficulty fitting some of the stones into his own mouth – he had kept some of the stones the girl had vomited, and was pleased to be able to show them to his relative and Mr Clerk. Mr Clerk in his letter to his friend says, 'I have sent you one, but not a quarter so big were some of them'. This behaviour lasted a fortnight and during that time many people came to witness it.

As well as the peculiar behaviour of ten-year-old Miss Stiff other things were happening too. Handfuls of flax which were thrown on the fire refused to burn, bed clothes would throw themselves off the bed – Moses himself had remade the bed several times, but the covers still came off. He then laid a Bible on top of the bed but that didn't make any difference and the Bible itself moved to another bed, and 'a strike of Wheat standing at the Beds feet, set it how they would, it would be thrown down again.' At one point so many things were flying round the room that nobody dare move for fear of being hit by something:

> In the Buttery the Milk would be taken off the Table, and set on the ground, and once one Panchion was broken, and the Milk Spilt. A seven pound weight with a ring was hung up on the Spigot, and the Beer mingled with the Sand and all spoiled, their Salt mingled perfectly with Bran.

Moses' mother described how flax was throw out of a box, even after putting it back in several times and locking the lid down on it: as soon as she turned her back the box became unlocked and it was thrown out again. Moses saw a loaf of bread fly off the table and a knife throw itself at a man who was passing by. All this time the stones kept coming and they were starting to fly round the rooms, breaking windows and hitting people who were outside the house. Luckily, 'no hurt was done to their persons'.

Mr Clerk ends his letter saying:

> At last some that had been long suspected for Witches were Examined, and one sent to the Gaol, where it is said she plays her pranks, but that is of doubtful credit. I asked the Old Woman whether they were free now. She said that one Night since, they heard great knockings and cruel noise, which scared them worse than all the rest, and once or twice that week her cheese was crumbled into pieces and spoiled.

Unfortunately we do not know the name of the woman who was suspected of witchcraft, nor at this time do we know what became of her.

ANNE DESBOROUGH

Anne Desborough was one of a group of people who were involved in the Huntingdon witchcraft trials of 1646. Anne was a widow living in Bythorn at the time, but the charge against her was from a time thirty years previously when had she lived at Titchmarsh, Northamptonshire. The evidence against her came from Thomas Becke of Bythorn, who took his oath before Nicholas Pedley Esq., a Justice of the Peace for Huntingdonshire, on the 9 April 1646. Mr Becke alleged that he, along with a Master Coyst and others, had heard Anne Desborough quite freely admit that while she was asleep in bed in her home in Titchmarsh: 'there appeared unto her a thing somewhat bigger than a mouse, of a brown colour, which nipped her on the breast and awakened her'.

It apparently told her that it had taken a bit of her soul, but after Anne prayed to God it disappeared. It returned five or six days later, this time with another mouse-like creature very similar to the first but with a white belly. The first 'mouse' told Anne that they needed to suck her blood and Anne agreed. Three days later they came to her again, this time saying that she must forsake God and that when she died they were to have her soul; all of this Anne agreed to. Mr Becke then when on to say that he had heard Anne say that she had given the name 'Tib' to one of the mice and 'Jone' to the other. Tib promised her that he could hurt men and Jone that he could hurt cattle whenever Anne wished it. Up until Anne was arrested there wasn't more than a twenty-four-hour period when they did not visit her and feed off her. At her trial Anne Desborough confessed that it was all true.

Church of the Holy Sepulchre.

THE COUNTY'S LINK TO SALEM

The most famous of the New World witchcraft trials took place in Salem, Essex County, Massachusetts between 1692 and 1693. It was centred around the extraordinary behaviour of a group of girls and young women aged between twelve and twenty who began having fits, making strange noises and contorting their bodies. It eventually escalated to the point where 156 people from 24 towns in the county were charged with witchcraft. A special court was set up to deal with the crisis, ending in the deaths of nineteen people by hanging and one fatality which occurred under interrogation.

Of the people involved in this trial special interest is focused on Giles Corey and his third wife Martha. Giles was born in Harpole around 1611, was baptised at the Holy Sepulchre church on 19 March, 1621 and took his family to America in about 1640 as an early colonial settler. Giles Corey is featured in Arthur Miller's play *The Crucible*.

The story starts on 20 January, 1692, when eleven year-old Abigail Williams and her cousin, nine year-old Elizabeth Parris, became the first to be affected by strange fits. This was quickly followed by eight other cases of the same hysterical behaviour. The local minister, Elizabeth's

THE CHURCH OF THE HOLY SEPULCHRE IS THE BEST PRESERVED OF ONLY FOUR REMAINING CIRCULAR CHURCHES IN ENGLAND BUILT BY RETURNING CRUSADERS ON THE MODEL OF JERUSALEM'S HOLY SEPULCHRE CHURCH. IT WAS BEGUN IN 1100 BY SIMON DE ST. LIZ; THE FIRST NORMAN EARL OF NORTHAMPTON, PROBABLY IN THANKS FOR THE SUCCESS OF THE FIRST CRUSADE AND HIS OWN SAFE RETURN. IT ORIGINALLY CONSISTED ONLY OF THE CIRCULAR NAVE AND A SMALL CHANCEL. A NORTH CHAPEL WAS ADDED AROUND 1200, AND TOWER IN THE 15TH CENTURY. THE BUILDING WAS FURTHER ENLARGED TO ITS PRESENT FORM IN THE 1860's.

PLACED BY NORTHAMPTON BOROUGH COUNCIL ·1988.

Sepulchre plaque.

father Samuel Parris, consulted with the other Church ministers to find a reason for their strange behaviour, but by mid-February, when no answers could be found, they called for the local doctor William Griggs. Griggs examined the girls but could find no medical reasons for their condition, finally stating that he believed it to be witchcraft.

It was decided that in order to cure the girls they would have to identify and punish the responsible party. The girls were questioned as to who was responsible for their bewitched state. The actual cause of the girl's condition is unknown, and many suggestions have been put forward over the years. They range from cereal disease, which infected their flour and caused hallucinations to general mischief on the girls' part, with one of the most popular suggestions being that the first two girls, Abigail and Elizabeth, became fascinated with stories of the occult and voodoo told by one of their servants, Tituba Indian, who had been brought by Revd Parris from Barbados. Either way, the girls were more than happy to go along with the witchcraft theory and quickly pointed the finger of suspicion at several local women.

The first to be accused was, not surprisingly, Tituba Indian, followed by Sarah Good, a beggar woman, and Sarah Osborne, an elderly cripple who had shocked the community years earlier by marrying her servant. All three were people on the fringe of society and did not attend the local church, making them a clever choice as there were few people who would defend them.

They were quickly arrested and brought before local magistrates John Hawthorne and Jonathan Corwin on the 1 March for a preliminary hearing. The women were questioned and their accusers were present during these interrogations. It was at this point that the trial took a very peculiar turn. The girls were standing in front of the accused some distance away when they started complaining of being bitten and pinched by them. The girls explained that it was the women's spectres pinching them and would often look around the courtroom and point as if they could see them.

To make matters worse for the accused, despite Sarah Good and Sarah Osborne denying any connection with witchcraft, Tituba openly confessed and identified both women as fellow witches with whom she had attended meetings. She went on to claim that a coven of witches operated in Massachusetts, led by a tall man dressed in black, and that she had been forced to sign a book in blood. Colonial America employed a similar legal system to Britain at this time and therefore her confession fulfilled one of the major conditions for proof of witchcraft, that of signing a pact with the Devil.

Tituba's confession and her talk of a coven struck fear into the hearts of the local community and this confession reinforced a series of rumours that had circulated a few years before that Salem Village would be destroyed by a group of witches and that the family of the local minister would be involved. The confession also led to the girls extending the range of the accused, although this is believed to have been helped by Mrs Thomas Putnam, the mother of Ann Putnam, one of the accusers.

The magistrates were also more than happy now to believe the girls, even more so than before, to the point of encouraging the girls to name others. No questions were asked when well-respected women in the village were accused. Among these were Martha Corey, a devout Christian and wife of local landowner Giles Corey who had publicly questioned the reliability of the evidence given by the afflicted girls, and Rebecca Nurse, who, like Martha, was well respected in the community and a regular churchgoer.

During Martha's examination before John Hawthorne the girls claimed to see a yellow bird suckling between her fingers and interrupted the proceedings with screams, claiming that they were being bitten, scratched and strangled by Corey's spectre. Ann Putnam also told Hawthorne that she had witnessed Corey praying to the Devil outside the window of the Putnam home. To add to Martha's plight, her husband had initially had testified against her, but later changed his opinion causing great suspicion among the townsfolk:

> The evidence of Giles Choree testifieth & saith that Last satturday in the Evening sitting by the fire my wife asked me to go to bed. I told I would go to prayr. & when I went to prayer I could nott utter my desires w'th any sense, not open my mouth to speake My wife did perceive itt & came towards. me & said she was coming to me. After this in alittle space I did according to my measure attend the duty. Sometime last weake I fetcht an ox well out the woods, about noone, & he laying down in the yard I went to raise him to yoake him butt he could not rise butt dragd his hinder parts as if he had been hiptshott, butt after did rise.
>
> I had a Catt somtimes last weeke strangly taken on the suddain & did make me think she would have died presently, [butt] my wife bid me knock her in the head. butt I did not. & since she is well. Another time going to duties I was interrupted for aspace, butt afftterward I was helpt according to my poore measure.
>
> My wife hath ben wont to sitt up after I went to bed, & I have perceived her to kneel down to the harth. as if she were at prayr, but heard nothing March: 24'th 1691/2.

As the hysteria increased more people began to claim, like Mrs Putnam, that they were attacked by the spectres, including John Indian, Tituba's husband. Many of these accusations of witchcraft were laced with elements of vengeance.

John and Elizabeth Proctor had upset the group of girls because while one of them, Mary Warren, had been a servant of the Proctors she started having fits and making accusations but these had mysteriously stopped after receiving a beating from her master. The other girls looked on this badly and quickly named Mary as a witch, therefore warning the other accusers not to change sides. Ironically Mary simply confirmed their accusations and was quickly welcomed back into the group, and Elizabeth Proctor was denounced as a witch on 3 April while her husband was arrested during her examination eight days later.

Even George Burroughs, the minister at the church in Salem from 1680 to 1682, was accused. Having once lodged with the Putnam family he had incurred their hostility. The girls accused him of having his spectre pinch and bite them, pointing out the fact that the bite marks matched the shape of his teeth. Even more damning for the preacher was the accusation that he had made some of them sign a book in blood supplied by the Devil, therefore signing a pact. He was also accused of making wax dolls and allowing them to stick pins in them and even murder. Burroughs, it was believed, was the head of the coven described by Tituba.

Accusation after accusation followed, finally leading to the county's own Giles Corey unsurprisingly being accused on 13 April and eventually certain of his wife's innocence, he had spoken out against the girls. Ann Putnam claimed that Corey's spectre had visited her and asked her to write her name in the Devil's book. This was later followed by Putnam claiming she had been visited by a ghost of someone who had been murdered by Corey. The other girls, not to be outdone, added that he was 'a dreadful wizard' and that they too had been assaulted by his spectre.

The court ordered his hands to be tied, then told him that it was not enough to, 'act witchcraft at other times, but must you do it now in face of authority?' to which he replied, 'I am a poor creature and cannot help it'. One of the magistrates asked, 'Why do you tell such wicked lies against witnesses?' At this point one of his hands was freed and the girls began to be afflicted. He held his head to one side, and the afflicted girls followed suit. He drew in his cheeks, and again this was mimicked.

Other accusations followed up until mid-May when the court was adjourned, as all the trials had only been preliminary and without a legitimate form of government, there was no way to try the accused legally. From their initial examinations all the accused had been committed to jail to await a full hearing. This process started when on 27 May the new governor Sir William Phips ordered a special 'Court of Oyer and Terminer' comprised of seven judges to try the witchcraft cases. By this time Sarah Osborne had died in jail without a trial, as had Sarah Good's newborn baby girl, and many others were ill.

By the time of Martha Corey's trial on 10 September, eleven people had been found guilty and hanged including Sarah Good, Rebecca Nurse, Reverend George Burroughs and John Proctor. However, Elizabeth Proctor was lucky enough to be released due to her pregnancy. Tituba Indian was also later released and exiled.

Martha Corey was found guilty and executed on 22 September, although she maintained her innocence to the last. The case of Giles Corey was not as straightforward. During the September trials his case was arraigned. Mercy Lewis's disposition, held at the Division of Archives and Records Preservation, Salem, states:

The Deposition of Mercy lewes agged about 19 years woh testifieth and saith that on the 14th April 1692 I saw the Apperishtion of Giles Cory com and aflect me urging me to writ in his book and so he contineued most dreadfullly to hurt me by times beating me & almost braking my back tell the day of his examination being the 19th April and then allso during the time

Henry Wadsworth Longfellow, Giles Corey of Salem Farms, in *The Poetical Works of Longfellow*, Houghton Mifflin Boston, 1902. Artist John W. Ehninger, 1880, p. 752.

of his examination he did affect and tortor me most greviously: and also several times sence urging me vehemently to writ in his book and I veryly believe in my heart that Giles Cory is a dreadfull wizzard for sence he had ben in prison he or his apperance has com and most greviously tormented me.' Seven other similar dispositions were given by the girls, with one piece of evidence saying 'the Spectre of Giles Corey Murdered his first wife & would have murdered this to if she had not been a Witch...

He was asked to plead guilty but refused to speak, so under the English law *peine forte et dure* (French for 'strong and hard punishment') he was:

remanded to the prison from whence he came and put into a low dark chamber, and there be laid on his back on the bare floor, naked, unless when decency forbids; that there be placed upon his body as great a weight as he could bear, and more, that he hath no sustenance, save only on the first day, three morsels of the worst bread, and the second day three droughts of standing water, that should be alternately his daily diet till he died, or, till he answered.

Giles Corey remained stubborn to the last, refusing to confess: as a result, English law could not try him. On 17 September Sheriff Corwin led him to a pit in an open field near the jail, stripped him and placed two boards on his chest. Six men lifted heavy stones onto his chest and stomach but, much to Corwin's dismay, Corey refused to cry out in pain, let alone confess.

After two days had passed he was asked three times to confess, each time asking for more weight to be added. Sheriff Corwin was known to stand on the stones from time to time and stare down at Corey's pained face. One witness Robert Calef later said, 'In the pressing, Giles Corey's tongue was pressed out of his mouth; the Sheriff, with his cane, forced it in again.' Finally Corey shouted out to Corwin, 'Damn you. I curse you and Salem!' Giles Corey died a few seconds later. Giles Corey's choice to 'stand mute' and endure death by such a harsh penalty is the only one in the history of New England where the law applied.

'Trial of Giles Corey – Giles Corey accused in court by one of the afflicted girls' in *A Popular History of the United States* by William Cullen Bryant, Vol. II, New York, Charles Scribner's Sons, 1878, p. 459. Artist: C.S. Reinhardt.

Fourteen years after the trials ended one of the girls, Ann Putnam, then aged twenty-six, confessed her fraud, asking her minister to read her confession at the Sunday service, 'It was a great delusion of Satan that deceived me in that sad time whereby I justly fear I have been instrumental to bring upon myself and this land the guilt of innocent blood.'

GREAT PAXTON

Accusations of witchcraft continued into the nineteenth century, including a case at Great Paxton in 1808. There had been a series of events that led up to this accusation, the parish records suggest that quite a few of the deaths that occurred around this time were unusual. John and Mary Hook had lost four of their seven children between 1790 and 1802, and of the three boys that survived one died just months after the attack on Ann Izzard, one of the suspected witches. Widow Alice Russell, another suspected witch, had lost her husband ten years before – he 'died in a fit at the bottom of the Hill, near the village' – two young lads had accidentally drowned, and in February 1808, just months before the first incident, a fourteen-year-old lad hanged himself, apparently, 'in a fit of lunacy'. It was then that a young girl by the name of Alice Brown started having fits. Given what had happened during the previous few years the villagers were quick to believe that she had been bewitched, and the finger was pointed at sixty-year-old Ann Izzard, a woman known to have a great knowledge of herbs and the suchlike, something which made people fear her. There had also been an incident where a driver of a wagonload of hay had refused to give her a lift up the hill, as a consequence she, 'cast a spell on him' and the wagon overturned. It was also said that she could be seen flying through the air on a broomstick. Two other girls, Fanny Amey and Mary Fox, also started to act as if they were 'bewitched', aAter the use of certain charms it was proven that Ann Izzard was to blame.

One Sunday night in May most of the villagers made their way to the home of Ann Izzard. Once there they surrounded the house, smashed down her door and dragged her naked from her bed into the yard. There they proceeded to knock her head against some stones, beat her with bits of wood and, in the true method of finding out if someone was a witch, prick her arms with pins. Finally, believing she was dead, they left her on the ground. Ann must have been one tough old lady, because she survived and managed to get herself back into her home, put on some clothes and get herself along to the local constable in the hope of protection. At that particular time the local constable was more likely to be a member of the local community and being so, refused to help her. That night Ann managed to find shelter in the home of Widow Russell, but the following night the violence was repeated and she was again pulled from the house, beaten and left for dead. Ann Izzard, against all odds, survived once again. The villagers were now absolutely certain that she was a witch – no one else could have survived such treatment. They decided the following night she would have to be ducked. Ann had other ideas however, and escaped during the day to the neighbouring village of Little Paxton, where she went to the rectory for protection. The Revd Nicholson was more than happy to aid the persecuted person and it is believed that she was moved on to St Neots. Back in the village of Great Paxton the villagers, deprived of the prospect of ducking a proper witch, turned their attention on Widow Russell, threatening her and charging her with aiding and abetting Ann Izzard. Within a fortnight of the first attack on her neighbour (with her health probably deteriorating under the pressure) Widow Russell died. Mary Hook was sent to prison for her part in the assaults on Ann Izzard, as was James Straughton, father of one of the boys that 'accidentally' drowned.

Great Paxton was described as, 'a small mean village, chiefly consisting of mud-walled and thatched cottages, the number of which, according to the returns of 1801, was 36, and that of the inhabitants 217.' In 1804, according to the Parish Register, 'a shilling was to be given to every poor person,' and widows and widowers were to get slightly more. More than half of the village were eligible for this charity payment, including the Izzards, Hooks, Ameys and Foxes.

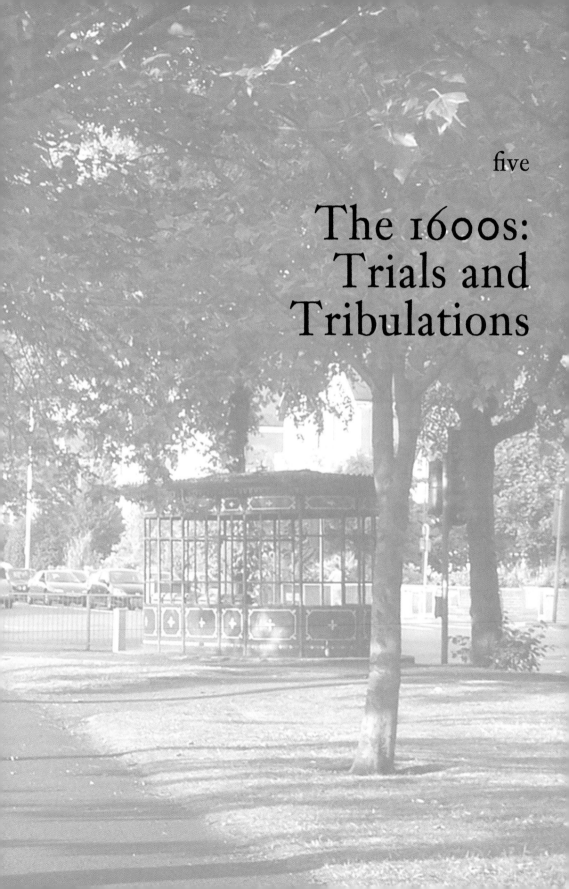

five

The 1600s: Trials and Tribulations

The start of the seventeenth century saw the end of forty-four years under the reign of Protestant Queen Elizabeth I and the start of the reign of James I (1603-1625), the first Stuart King of England and Ireland. King James wasn't a popular monarch and the 1605 Gunpowder Plot was indeed an attempt to get rid of him. If it hadn't been for the fact that Francis Tresham's father had died in the September of that year, delaying the blast date by two months, who knows how the century would have turned out. As it was, the seventeenth century was full of upheaval with changing religions, politics, food shortages, Civil War and general unrest amongst the people.

From 1603 enclosure of the land had been proposed but it was in 1607 that King James, needing to raise money for the royal coffers, started selling off Crown property, usually to the squires of the counties. This caused a great deal of resentment amongst the ordinary people because they suddenly found themselves without a home as the land was fenced off. The 'Midland riot' began in Northamptonshire, where there had been signs of unrest from 1604. Sir Thomas Tresham was one of the people in Northamptonshire who purchased land around his home village of Newton. Trees were felled, ground cleared, hedges and fences erected and sheep were bought in to replace the people on the land. Not surprisingly, the local 'peasants' who had lived, farmed and raised families on this land decided to fight back, these were the 'Levellers'. As the land was enclosed and their houses were taken from them, they began to rip up hedges and destroy the fences – John Reynolds, with his superstitious 'pouch,' being a leader of such men.

It wasn't just an act of wanton violence. They had a lot of support – the clergy even preached about the suffering of the families involved – but eventually news reached the King in London. On 30 May 1607 a royal proclamation instructed the Lord Lieutenants of the county to, 'immediately suppress (the levellers) by whatever means they may, be in force of arms if other lawful means do not serve and reduce them to their duties.' On the 8 June it all came to a head with the lieutenants and every servant that they could reliably arm facing the Levellers. The battle was short-lived and the lieutenants came through victorious. The ringleaders were tried and executed, and although no record exists of what happened to John Reynolds there is a document believed to be still in existence that has the names of 143 people who signed with the promise that this would never happen again.

All across the county things were changing, with the 'peasants' often living hand to mouth. (It's probably no wonder that superstition and witchcraft became rife). People during this time were incredibly superstitious and it was very easy to believe in witchcraft especially when crops failed, animals died and plagues and pestilence swept back and forth across the country wiping out whole families with no apparent explanation. People needed entertainment and looked forward to feast-day celebrations, but even these could be under threat from the Puritan landowners. One such event occurred on 18 July 1618 at Grafton Underwood.

St James's Day (named in honour of the local church) was celebrated on the 25 July, and as was often the case tended to last two or three days. Two local landowners and Justices of the Peace, Sir Edward Montagu and his neighbour Sir Thomas Brooke of Oakley, had other ideas, and tried to subdue the approaching feast by issuing a warrant to the constable of Grafton Underwood. It stated that no unlicensed beer should be sold (it was a common practice for people to brew their own), that any fiddlers coming from any outside villages without prior consent, 'should be dealt with as rogues,' and that anyone who, 'used any unlawful recreations before the end of devine service on the Sundays or Holy days' should be severely punished. Finally, anyone who came from any of the surrounding villages was to be refused access, if these people refused to go home then they were 'to be proceeded against according to the statutes and his Majesty's pleasure.'

Luckily for the villagers, they had a saviour in the form of the newly appointed parson, Dr Williams. Dr Williams, himself a Justice of the Peace, disagreed strongly with everything written in the warrant, and standing in the churchyard before that evening's service he told the villagers that if the 'alewives' wanted to sell their beer then they should, if they wanted fiddlers to play then so be it and if there were none in the village then they could send for some from elsewhere. If strangers wanted to join in the festivities then they should do and furthermore, 'you shall use your pastimes and your sports'. Having said his piece, he then went back to his house and made a copy of the warrant. He then asked several people to witness that it was indeed a true copy. From depositions taken from the villagers of Grafton Underwood by Sir Thomas Brooke and Sir John Pickering, Esq., of Titchmarsh just after the feast it seems Dr Williams got his way.

WITCHCRAFT AT ITS PEAK

Although there is no doubt that witch trials took place both before and after the seventeenth century, nothing seems to compare to the amount that actually took place during it – so much so they became almost a national pastime, becoming so commonplace that they were by and large ignored by the general populace. Consequently, very few trials were actually recorded for posterity.

This chapter recounts the trials for which information is still available today. The county's story starts with Agnes Browne, who has the dubious honour of being the first person in Northamptonshire to be arrested and convicted on charges of witchcraft in the seventeenth century.

Agnes Browne and Joane Vaughan

Agnes Browne of Guilsborough was born to a poor family and a poor education. This led to her apparently being, 'of an ill nature and wicked disposition, spiteful and malicious'. Because of this, she was feared and hated by her neighbours. Agnes had an unmarried daughter, Joane (spelt Ioane in the seventeenth century) Vaughan or Varnham, who, it seems, inherited her mother's temperament. Joane grew up very much under her mother's wing, preferring her company to that of the other residents of the village.

Elizabeth Belcher.

One day while walking through the village Joane came across 'Mistris' Belcher, a God-fearing woman, in conversation with others and, whether deliberately or not, she caused offence either verbally or through gesticulation to such a degree that Miss Belcher felt it so unbecoming of a woman that she struck her. This was not meant to hurt her but more as a means to remove her from their company. Joane became so furious that she swore revenge, however, Miss Belcher was heard to answer her saying, 'she feared neither her nor her mother', and told her to do her worst.

Joane rushed home to her mother and told her the story. Agnes and her daughter decided it would be best to wait a few days so as not to raise suspicion before they exacted their revenge. A few days later Miss Belcher was struck by such intolerable pain that she took to her bed, and her face became so disfigured it frightened all her visitors. During this time she was heard to cry, 'here comes Joane Vaughan, away with Joane Vaughan'.

For a long time she remained in this aggravated state, much to the amazement of her friends. It is believed that during this period she was treated by Dr John Cotta, though to no avail and finally, her brother Master Avery, hearing of his sister's pain, came to visit. He was taken by his sister's plight but not knowing the nature of her illness was helpless to find a cure, all the time hearing his sister cry out the witches' names. He decided to confront Agnes and Joane, but when he reached their house he became stuck to spot, motionless either through fear or enchantment. Three times Avery tried to confront the witches at their home, but every time he became rooted to the same spot: extremely despondent, he returned to his home, where he hoped he would be safe from the witches' evil. Unfortunately, like his sister, he too was struck with 'fits'. These lasted until the witches were arrested by Sir William Saunders of 'Codesbrooke' (Cottersbrooke) and taken to Northampton 'Gaole' (Gaole is a seventeenth-century word meaning jail).

The brother and sister then went to Northampton to scratch the witches. This was at the time thought to remove the power from the witches, thus removing the curse. While they were in the presence of the witches this seem to work, but once out of their sight, the fits returned, only this time more violently. They then took a coach to return home, but on the way they spotted

Guilsborough witches riding a pig (cover of a Taylor & Sons pamphlet, 1612).

a man and a woman riding on a black horse. Avery saw them gesturing to him, and stopped to speak to them. It was then that the horses dropped down dead.

Avery saw this as a sign from God that instead of hurting them, the witches' fury had been turned against the horses instead. After this, according to a pamphlet printed at the time, they hurried home praising God and were never troubled again.

At the arraignment, Agnes Browne and Joan Vaughan were indicted for bewitching Miss Belcher and her brother Master Avery, as well as for the murder of an unknown young child. They pleaded not guilty on all counts, and although they protested their innocence to the last the court found them guilty and the execution was carried out on 22 July, 1612.

There is another story regarding these witches and it is said that two weeks before their arrest Agnes Browne, Katherine Gardiner and Joane Lucas rode upon a sow's back from Guilsborough to Ravensthorpe to visit an old witch called 'mother' Rhodes. It is said that before they got to the old witch's home she died, crying out in her last breath that three of her old friends are coming to visit but they will be too late, 'Howbeit shee would meete with them in another place within a month after'. Whether this was witch's foresight or just coincidence no one will ever know.

Guilsborough parish records show that Agnes Varnam married Thomas Browne on 1 November 1581. Thomas was buried at Guilsborough in 1583, the same year Joane was baptised, and this may well explain the confusion over daughter Joane's surname. A woodcut of this story depicting the three witches on the sow's back can be seen on the cover of the pamphlet *The witches of Northamptonshire printed by Thomas Purfoot for Arthur Johnson in 1612.*

Mary Barber

It was said that Mary Barber of Stanwick was born to such mean parents that she was, 'monstrous and hideous, both in her life, and actions'. She dressed poorly, spoke rudely, had violent tendencies and no education to speak of and was described as, 'never promising anything to the world'.

She was arrested on 6 May 1612 by Sir Thomas Tresham for bewitching a man to death and harming cattle and taken to Northampton gaol. Little is known of the trial but Mary was found guilty and sentenced to death. A pamphlet printed by Taylor & Son on Northamptonshire in the mid-nineteenth century states:

> Mary Barber, of Stanwicke, was one in whom the licentiousness of her passions grew to bee the master of her reason, and did so conquer in her strength and power of all virtue, that shee fell to the apostacy of goodnesse, and became diverted, and abused unto most vilde actions, cloathing her desperate soule in the most ugly habiliments that either malice, envy or cruelty could produce from the blindnesse of her degenerate and Devilish desires.

Helen Jenkenson

Helen Jenkenson of Thrapston was suspected of being evil a long time before her apprehension for 'bewitching cattle and other mischiefes'. Sir Thomas Brooke arrested Helen on 11 May 1612 for bewitching a child to death and imprisoned her in Northampton Gaol.

Just before her arrest a 'Mistris' Moulsho discreetly inspected Helen Jenkenson for marks that, 'all witches have in some privy place or other' and it is said to her amazement she found some. At that time Miss Moulsho had just put her clothes ready for washing. The next morning, when the maid went to hang them up to dry, she noticed that all the clothes were, 'bespotted with pictures of Toades, Snakes and other ougly Creatures'. She reported to her mistress straight away, but to her amazement, she just smiled and said simply: 'Heere are fine Hobgoblins indeed.' Being a stern woman with little fear, she rushed to the house of Helen Jenkenson and angrily told her that if she didn't clean her linen of all the spots she would scratch both her eyes out and without waiting for an answer she returned home, whereupon she found 'her linnen as white as it was at first.'

Other than this story little can be found in relation to the actual charge of bewitching a child to death! When bought before the court and charged, Helen pleaded not guilty, but to her shock was found guilty; she, like Arthur Bill, shouted at the court that she was, 'as innocent as the rest' and refused to confess or show remorse. Up until the last she stood strong. Helen Jenkenson was hanged on 22 July, 1612.

Arthur Bill

Arthur Bill was born and lived in Raunds, 'a wretched poore Man, both in state and mind'. His parents were both said to have been witches and Arthur welcomed this, happy to listen to his father's teachings.

The crime for which he stood trial was that of bewitching to death the body of Martha Aspine alias Jeames, the daughter of Edward Aspine, also of Raunds. At the time there were fears as to whether Arthur Bill would be found guilty as he had previously been cleared of bewitching cattle, and although there was no actual evidence that he had committed this crime the general public feared the power of Arthur and his parents. The justices and officials had the father, mother and son bound, with their thumbs and toes tied together, and ducked. All three of them floated on the water. This confirmed them as witches, and Arthur being the main part of the trial was sent to Northampton Gaol on 29 May 1612 by Sir Gilbert Pickering of Titchmarsh.

Arthur, fearing his father might confess under the strain, sent for his mother to visit him. The story goes that after Arthur had told her of his fears he joined with his mother and manifested a round ball in the mouth of the father making it impossible for him to speak. This, unfortunately for Bill, didn't help, as his father proved to be the principal witness in the case against him.

During the trial Arthur's mother, fearing being hanged, fainted many times; she complained to her guardian spirit that the power of the law was greater than her powers of witchcraft, and that she should be hanged as her son was likely to be. The spirit is said to have told her she would not hang, but she should cut her own throat. Hearing that she would die anyway she fell to the ground ranting and raving, cursing the day she was born.

Her neighbours, often hearing these so-called conversations with the spirit, told her to pray to God and ask forgiveness for her sins, but she would hear none of it and after tormenting herself for three or four days, she followed the Devil's advice and slit her own throat. Hearing of his mother's suicide and his father's betrayal at becoming a witness against him, Arthur became frustrated. The one person he trusted and confided in was dead and the person he feared most, his father, had turned against him. He stuck resolutely by his pledge of innocence.

Proof was supplied against him that he had unknowingly confessed to having spirits working for him who would, at his command, 'doe any mischiefe to any man, woman or child that hee would appoint'. It was said, possibly by his father, that he had three spirits working for him; he gave them each special names, 'The Diuell [Devil] himselfe sure was godfather to them all, the first hee called Grissill, the other was named Ball, and the last Jacke'. It is not known in what form these spirits materialised.

Arthur remained in his cell from 29 May until 22 July, all the time adamant he was innocent, despite many visits asking him to confess and pray to God for forgiveness. At the assizes he was charged with the murder of Martha Aspine as well as several other crimes he was said to have committed. He was found guilty, at this time crying out that, 'he had found the law to have a power above justice, for that it had condemned an innocent'.

Even as he was standing on the stage at his execution he pleaded his innocence to the last. There is an entry in the Raunds parish records which says 'Martha Aspine a Jeames buried 16th June 1624', so was Arthur innocent after all?

The 1612 Trials

All five prisoners were brought from the town gaol to Northampton Castle, where the assizes were usually held, and pleaded not guilty, yet all were found guilty and sentenced to death by the jury. On 22 July 1612 they were all sent to Abington gallows and hanged. It is of note that not only were all five convicted of being witches and all vehemently protested their innocence but they all shared the common denominator of being of poor birth and education. It is fortunate that this quirk of fate is not subject to such persecution today!

Ann Foster

The century draws to a close with the only other recorded case on file, that of one Ann Foster of Eastcote. Very little information on this trial is available, but from the documents that do exist Ann was described as, 'an old woman who had long been observed muttering to herself'. She was accused and found guilty of bewitching horses, cattle and sheep belonging to Joseph Weedon, also from Eastcote, as well as with, 'Satan her colleague, set his house and barns on Fire'.

One account of her stay in jail, taken from a pamphlet printed at the time, quotes:

The keepers caused her to be chained to a Post that was in the Gaol; but she had not been long so tied before she began to swell in all parts of her body, that her skin was ready to burst, which caused her to cry out in the most lamentable manner, insomuch that they were forced to Unchain her again, and to give her more Liberty that the Devil might come to suck her, which he usually did, coming constantly about the dead time of night in the likeness of a Rat, which at his coming, made the most lamentable and hideous noise which affrighted the people which did belong to the Gaol, which caused many to come and see her during her abode there, and

Joseph Weedon.

several hath been with her when the Devil hath been coming to her, but could see nothing but things like Rats, and heard a most terrible noise.

The only other known information available comes from a lecture on witchcraft in Northamptonshire given by the Revd J. Jackson Goadby, F. G. S. of Henley-on-Thames in the Town Hall at Northampton during the mid-nineteenth century. He made the following speech:

The Eastcote case shows us what in the days of Charles the second were the consequences of dear mutton. A well-to-do farmer at Eastcote, near Foster's Booth, killed a sheep for his own household. An old woman, muttering and grumbling, and perhaps hungry, came to his house, offered money, but not enough for a joint, and went away threatening the farmer. Mutton was then very dear and scarce, and the farmer didn't think he had asked too much. Some days after the woman called, 30 sheep were found dead, legs broken and other bones broken 'every bone in their bodies indeed'. His neighbours 'came and saw,' and gave it as their opinion that the sheep had been bewitched, and advised that one of the dead sheep should be burnt. The farmer took their advice. The sheep, however wouldn't burn; and then came up the old crone who had offered to buy his mutton, and complained of his folly in trying to burn a sheep. The farmer saw at once who was the cause of his loss, seized a knife, gave her a cut over her head, fetched blood, and the woman went off, threatening the farmer with arrest for his cut. Being a quiet man the farmer gave the woman 20s to pay the doctor. The woman said he had given her devils' money, and that she'd now pay him out. Presently after some days, his house and barns were on fire. The old crone again appeared on the scene, and told the neighbours that it was in vain to try and put out the fire. The neighbours seized her, took her to a Justice of the Peace, who sent her to Northampton Jail. Here she was chained to a post, but had to be unchained because she began to swell out, like the Poodle in the chamber of Faust. Every night the Devil, in the shape of a rat, came to her, the said rat 'making Lamentable and hideous noises,' and afflicting the people who belonged in prison. The poor creature was tried, confessed that the Devil provoked her, and was hanged – not for setting fire to the farmer's house, but for bewitching his sheep when mutton was dear and scarce.

Ann was hanged as a witch on 22 August, 1674.

Other witches

There is reference to two other witches in the county during the 1600s. Unfortunately, there are no details regarding them other than a few short sentences, but for reasons of completeness we provide what information there is.

During the late 1660s Judge Sir Richard Rainsford of Dallington had a witch bought before him. A knight (alas, we do not know his name) came to say that if, 'she were let off his estate would not be worth anything'. It seems the witch was let off, much to the dismay of the knight, who became so upset that the judge ordered the witch to be kept at the town's expense in the gaol at a cost of half a crown a week.

The other very short reference involved Judge Sir William Montague (son of Sir Edward Montague, Justice of the Peace) who tried many popish plotters and sentenced to death Alicia Welland, one of the last witches to be executed in England.

1705 – THE LAST EXECUTION!

Contrary to the popular belief that witches were burnt at the stake, evidence shows that this was not the case in Northamptonshire. Hanging was the preferred method, although there were two exceptions to this rule, namely Elinor Shaw and Mary Phillips – who also, if evidence can be believed, were the last two people to be executed for their 'beliefs' in England. Elinor was born at Cottestock to parents who, at the time, were described as 'obscure', and who didn't seem to care one way or another about their daughter; consequently, she received little or no education and by the age of fourteen was fending for herself. It was about this time that she met Mary Phillips from the neighbouring village of Oundle. They apparently continued a harmless friendship up until Elinor turned twenty-one, when things took a turn for the worse.

Elinor started behaving in an extraordinary manner, exposing herself to any man who would give her a second glance, gaining for herself such a reputation that she was talked about not only in her own village but in the neighbouring ones of Oundle, Glapthorn, Benefield, Southwick and several others. It got so bad that even children as young as four or five would jeer at her as soon as she stepped foot out of her door, calling out such things as, 'There goes a whore, there's Nell the Strumpet,' which not unnaturally made Elinor worse, and, 'being naturally of a Chollerick Disposition,' (together with her old friend Mary, 'who was as bad as her self in the Vices') she swore revenge on all their enemies. What follows is their story.

Elinor Shaw and Mary Phillips

On Wednesday 7 March 1705, on the second day of the assizes held at Northampton, Elinor Shaw and Mary Phillips were brought before the court on several indictments of witchcraft. They were accused of bewitching and tormenting the wife of Robert Wise of Benefield until she had died, killing by witchcraft four-year-old Elizabeth Gorham of Glapthorn, and bewitching Charles Ireland of Southwick to death. Both women pleaded not guilty and were therefore put on trial.

The first indictment against them was the case of Mrs Wise, and evidence against them came from one Widow Peak, who said that (along with another two women) she had watched the prisoners after they were apprehended, and that around midnight, 'a little white thing' appeared in the room about the size of a cat. It sat upon Mary Phillips' lap, at which time she heard Mary Phillips say, while pointing to Elinor Shaw, that she was the witch who had killed Mrs Wise by roasting wax effigies of her and sticking them with pins. Mrs Evans was second on the stand and stated that on New Year's Eve, when Mrs Wise was first taken ill, she saw Elinor Shaw look out of window, which was opposite her house, and say, 'I have done her business now I am sure, this night I'll send the old Devil a new year's gift'. Knowing Elinor Shaw was reputed to be a witch she felt concerned about her words and went to see how Mrs Wise was. When she arrived at the victim's house she found her tormented with pain, which increased to such a terrible degree that at midnight she died.

Further evidence given by Mrs Evans at the trial was that while they were at the house of Mrs Wise, Elinor Shaw and Mary Phillips had told her she was a fool to live such a miserable life, and that if she was willing, they would send something to relieve her that night. The woman foolishly agreed, and that very night, 'two little black things, almost like moles' came into her bed and sucked at the lower parts of her body. This continued for the following two or three nights until the woman became so frightened that she sent for the local minister, Mr Danks, to pray for her. Before the so-called imps left her, she added that she had heard the prisoners say that they would get revenge on Mrs Wise, because they had refused to give them some buttermilk (the popular belief being that the imps fed on buttermilk).

The next case was that of the unfortunate Charles Ireland. Evidence was given by Mrs Todd of Southwick, who described the misfortune that struck twelve-year-old Charles. She described how Charles was struck with strange fits the Christmas before, and how after twelve days of slow deterioration he began to bark like a dog. During this time Charles distinctly described Elinor Shaw and Mary Phillips and blamed them for his misfortunes, even though he claimed never seen them before in his life. At this point Charles' mother was advised to cork some of his urine in a stone bottle filled with pins and needles and bury it under the hearth of the fire. With this done the said witches came to the house and asked for the bottle to be removed. Mrs Ireland refused, and the witches confessed to bewitching the boy and promised not to do it again, but two evenings later Charles died. This testimony was then confirmed by five or six other people.

The witches were tried a third time for, 'bewitching to death' Elizabeth Gorham of Glapthorn, on the 10 February the previous year, as well as killing several horses, hogs and sheep belonging to Matthew Gorham, the deceased's father. This evidence was provided by two local constables, William Boss and John Southwel. While Elinor Shaw and Mary Philips were in their custody the constables threatened them with death if they did not confess and promised to release them if they did. After some forceful persuasion, both witches made a confession to the constables.

What follows is the confession given to the constables as is appeared in the pamphlet *An account of the Tryals, Examination and Condemnation of Elinor Shaw, and Mary Phillips, & c. by Ralph Davis, March 8 1705*:

That living in one house together they contracted with the Devil about a year ago, to sell their souls to him, upon condition, he would enable them to do what mischief they desired, against whom they pleased, either in body, goods or children; upon which the same night, they had each of them three imps sent as they were going to bed, and at the same instant the Devil appeared to them in the shape of a tall black man, and told them, that these imps would always be at their services, either to kill man, woman, child, hog, cow, ship [sheep], or any other creature, when they pleased to command them, provided they let 'em suck their flesh every night; which being agreed to, the Devil came to bed them both, and had carnal knowledge of 'em, as if a man, only with this difference instead of being warm, his embraces were very cold and unpleasant. And that the next morning they sent four imps to kill two horses of one John Webb of the said town of Glapthorn, because he openly said they were witches, and accordingly the horses were found dead in a pond the same day; and two days after this they kill'd four great hoggs after the same manner belonging to Matthew Gorham, because he said they both look'd like witches, and not thinking this revenge sufficient, the next day after they sent two imps a piece to destroy his child being a little girl of about four years of age, which was done accordingly in 24 hours time not withstanding all the skill and endeavour of able doctors to preserve it; they further confessed that if the said imps were not constantly imploy'd to do mischief they had not their healths, but when they were imploy'd they were very healthful and well. They further added, that the said imps did not often tell them in the night-time, in a holow whispering low voice which they plainly understood, that they should never feel hell torments, and that they had kill'd a horse and two cows of the widdow Broughton because she deny'd them some peascods [peascods are peas in their pods] last year, for which they had also struck her daughter with lameness, which would never be cured as long as either of them liv'd, and accordingly she has continued so ever since.

There was further information regarding the pact they made with the Devil contained in a letter written by Ralph Davis to a friend. On Saturday 12 February 1704, at about midnight, the Devil appeared in the form of a tall dark man. Both women were startled, but were assured by the Devil that they should not fear him. He took Elinor's hand and told her, 'I am one of the Creation as well as your selves, having the power given me to bestow it on whom I please, and do assure you, that if you will pawn your souls to me for only a Year and two Months, I will for all that time assist you in whatever you desire.' It is then recorded that he produced a piece of parchment, and with their own blood, obtained by pricking their fingers, the contract was written and signed. He then took them to bed where he had his wicked way with them, and in the morning he informed them they were now worthy of being witches and that they should use the imps to assist them in whatever way they required.

After extracting the said confession the constables persuaded the prisoners to sign it with their mark, apparently with much difficulty. Having been shown in court and in front of ten witnesses who swore they had heard the confession, the document was then produced as evidence at the hearing, but both witches denied that it was their confession or that it was their marks. Elinor Shaw and Mary Phillips then began howling with laughter, much to the amazement of the court, denying every charge brought against them. However the court, having weighed up all the facts of the trial and feeling the evidence overwhelming, especially the signed confession, found the prisoners guilty of 'willful' murder and witchcraft. The following day the court pronounced the death sentence.

The day before the execution was due to take place they were visited by the local minister, Mr Danks, in the hope they would show some degree of repentance. However, this was not to be the case. The minister, in the hope of understanding, then asked them to explain their dealings

Above and opposite: Site of the gallows at the racecourse on the corner of Kingsley Park Terrace and Kettering Road.

with the Devil. After conferring, Elinor told him that the Devil had appeared several times to them, always in the guise of a tall dark man, and on each occasion presenting them with new imps of different colours varying from red to black, 'and that these infernal Imps did nightly Suck each of them a large Teat, or pieces of red Flesh in their Privy Parts'. Elinor then went on to brag about the actual numbers affected by their witchcraft in a nine-month period, stating that they had killed fifteen children, eight men and six women, although at the time none of these deaths had been attributed to witchcraft. They also listed forty hogs, one hundred sheep, eighteen horses and thirty cows, proud of the fact that this resulted in the ruin of more than one family.

There is also a record of a couple of incidents that occurred whilst they were in prison, the first concerning a Mr Laxton and his wife. It seems while peering through the cell bars at Elinor, Mrs Laxton was heard to remark that the Devil had abandoned them as he was known to do with all his lackeys – at which point Elinor was seen mumbling in an unknown language for several minutes, following which Mrs Laxtons' clothes started acting in such a strange manner that her skirts flew up over her head leaving her exposed and embarrassed. Mr Laxton valiantly tried to right his wife's clothing but to no effect and it was only after Elinor had had a good laugh and told Mrs Laxton that she was a liar that her clothes returned to their normal place. The other incident involved none other than the keeper of the prison, who had threatened to clap them in irons; this was not appealing to either of the women, so, much to the amazement of the rest of the prison, the keeper was forced to dance naked in the prison yard for almost an hour. It appears that it was very unwise to taunt these women in their presence.

An extract from an eyewitness account taken from *Executions in Northampton* by an anonymous author states the following:

They were hardened in their wickedness that they publicly boasted that their master (meaning the Devil) would not suffer them to be executed, but they found him a liar, for on Saturday morning, being the 17th inst., they were carried to the gallows on the north side of town, whither numerous crowds of people went to see them die, and being come to the place of execution the minister repeated his former pious endeavours, to bring them to sense of their sins, but to as little purpose as before; for instead of calling upon God for mercy, nothing was heard of them but damning and cursing; however, a little before they tied up, at the request of the minister, Elinor Shaw confessed not only the crime for which she dyed but openly declared before them all how she first became a witch, as did also Mary Phillips; and being desired to say their prayers, they both set up a very loud laughter, calling for the Devil to come and help them in such a blasphemous manner as is not fit to mention; so that the sheriff seeing their presumptious impenitence, caused them to be executed with all the expedition possible, even while they were cursing and raving, and as they lived the Devil true factors, so they resolutely dyed in his service to the terror of all the people who were eye witnesses to their dreadful and amazing exits.

So that being Hang'd till they were almost Dead, the fire was put to the Straw, Faggots and other Combustable matter, till they were Burnt to Ashes. Thus Liv'd and thus Dyed, two of the most notorious and presumptious Witches, that ever were known in this Age.

Bibliography

Antiquarian Memoranda XXX: a series of lectures by Revd J. Jackson Goadby, the *Northampton Guardian,* 1880

Cotta, John, *The Trial of Witchcraft,* George Puralowe, London, 1616

Cowley, Richard, *Guilty M'Lud! The criminal history of Northamptonshire,* Kettering, Northamptonshire, 1998

Cunningham, Scott, *Wicca: A Guide for the Solitary Practitioner,* Llewellyn Publications, Minnesota, USA, 2004

Cunningham, Scott, *The Complete Book of Incense, Oils & Brews,* Llewellyn Publications, Minnesota, USA, 2004

Earle, Alice Morse, *Curious Punishments of Bygone Days,* Chicago, USA, 1896

Fell Smith, Charlotte, *John Dee: 1527-1608,* Constable and Company, London, 1909

Fraser, Antonia, *King James VI of Scotland and James I of England,* Weidenfeld and Nicolson, London, 1974

Geddes & Grosset, *Witchcraft,* Geddes & Grosset, New Lanark, Scotland, 2005

Gotch, A., *The Old halls and Manor Houses of Northamptonshire,* 1936

Guiley, Rosemary Ellen, *The Encyclopedia of Witches and Witchcraft,* Facts on File, New York, 1989

Harrison, Paul, *Northampton Murders,* Countryside Books, Berkshire, 1991

Hopkins, James, *The Discovery of Witches,* England, 1647

King, Frances X., *Witchcraft and Demonology,* Hamlyn Publishing Group Ltd, Middlesex, 1987

King James I, *Daemonologie,* England, 1597

Kramer, Heinrich and Springer, James, *Malleus Maleficarum [Hammer of the Witches],* 1486

Pipe, Marian, *Northamptonshire Stories,* Countryside Books, Berkshire, 1995

Radford, E. and M.A., *The Encyclopedia of Superstitions,* revised by Christina Hole, Helicon Publishing Ltd, Oxford, England, 1995

Renton, Ethel and Eleanor, *Records of Guilsborough, Nortoft, and Hollowell, Northamptonshire,* Bridewell Printing Works, Kettering 1929

Saint, David, *Northamptonshire Tales of Murder & Mystery,* Countryside Books, Berkshire, 2005

Scot, Reginald, *Discoverie of Witchcraft,* England, 1584

Serjeantson, Revd K.M., *The Castle of Northampton, Printed by Joseph Tebbutt, Corner of King Street,* 1908

Stearne, John, *A Confirmation and Discovery of Witchcraft,* 1648

The Macmillan Encyclopedia 1996

Willson, David Harris, *King James VI & I,* Oxford University Press, Oxford, 1956

The following are from the Northamptonshire Archives:

Northamptonshire Bedside Book: A collection of Prose and Poetry, The Dovecote Press Ltd, Dorset, 2002
Northamptonshire Image, January 1992
Northamptonshire Notes and Queries, Vol. I & Vol. II, 1886
Northampton Mercury, 1 August 1785
Northamptonshire Papers, Printed and Published by Taylor & Son, 1879
Northampton Past and Present, Vol I, The Northamptonshire Records Society, Lamport Hall, 1948
Northampton Past and Present, Vol. IV No. 3, The Northamptonshire Records Society, Lamport Hall, 1948
Relation of a Memorable Piece of Witchcraft, Printed & Published by Taylor & Son, 1867
The Diary of Thomas Isham of Lamport, translated by N. Marlow, originally written 1671-1673
The Northampton Mercury Reprints in 'Things old and new, in questions and answers',
16 Oct 1886-5 Nov 1887
Taylor & Son Pamphlet, reprinted 1867
Taylor & Son Pamphlet, printed 1866 – *A Brief History of Witchcraft*.
The Witches of Northamptonshire, Printed by Tho: Purfoot, for Arthur Johnson, London, 1612

Other local titles published by Tempus

Memories of Milton Keynes
MARION HILL

Many changes have taken place in Milton Keynes over the last forty years and it is the people, whose experiences are recorded here, who have shaped the area into the remarkable city it is today. All contributions come from the oral archive kept at the Living Archive of Milton Keynes, which has been collecting reminiscences from city residents since 1975, and are complemented by 100 photographs from their collection.

0 7524 3397 0

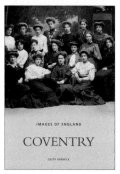

Coventry
GEOFF BARWICK

Once a medieval walled city, Coventry has thrived as home to a variety of industries, from the weaving and dying of cloth and silks to watchmaking in the eighteenth century and the boom in the construction of motor cars in the twentieth century. This fascinating volume of over 200 photographs and illustrations, the vast majority never before published, offers a unique glimpse into the history of Coventry over the past 150 years.

0 7524 3533 7

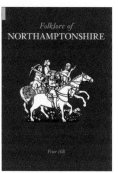

Folklore of Northamptonshire
PETER HILL

Northamptonshire is a place of contrasts. Especially rich in traditions, dialect and vocabulary, legends, and wondrous stories that have been handed down through the ages, the character of Northamptonshire and its people is firmly rooted in its folklore. This illustrated study of folklore rediscovers those traditions and the beliefs, stories, maxims and superstitions of daily life, as well as music and verse, dance and song.

0 524 3522 1

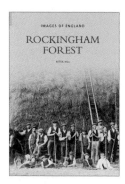

Rockingham Forest
PETER HILL

This absorbing collection of old images offers a nostalgic glimpse into the remarkable past of Rockingham Forest, which at one time covered almost half of the county of Northamptonshire. Accompanied by informative text, providing a wealth of local colour and historical detail, Rockingham Forest will delight all those who know the towns and fifty-eight villages of the Forest, whether they are long-time residents, newcomers or tourists to the the area.

0 7524 3640 6

If you are interested in purchasing other books published by Tempus, or in case you have difficulty finding any Tempus books in your local bookshop, you can also place orders directly through our website

www.tempus-publishing.com